WELCOME!

On behalf of Splash! Publications, we would like to welcome you to *The Civil War*, one of several books in our American History series. Since this curriculum was designed by teachers, we are positive that you will find it to be the most comprehensive program you have ever utilized to teach students about the Civil War. We would like to take a few moments to familiarize you with the program.

THE FORMAT

The Civil War is a 13 lesson program. Our goal is a curriculum that you can use the very first day you purchase our materials. No lessons to plan, comprehension questions to write, activities to create, or vocabulary words to define. Simply open the book and start teaching.

Each of the 13 lessons requires students to complete vocabulary cards, read about a Civil War event, and complete a Reading comprehension activity that will expose them to various standardized test formats. In addition, each lesson includes a balanced mix of lower and higher level activities for students to complete. Vocabulary quizzes, thought provoking discussion questions, mapping activities that use intermediate directions, reference points, and grid systems, research projects and journal writing activities utilizing graphic organizers, and primary sources are the types of activities that will guide students through their journey of *The Civil War*.

THE LESSON PLANS

On the next several pages, you will find the Lesson Plans for *The Civil War*. The Lesson Plans clearly outline what students must do before, during, and after each lesson. Page numbers are listed so that you will immediately know what you need to photocopy before beginning each lesson. The answers to all activities, quizzes, and comprehension questions are located on pages 111-118.

NOTE: Students will complete a culminating activity at the end of the curriculum. We suggest that students keep the information from each lesson in a notebook or folder.

THE VOCABULARY

Each lesson features words in bold type. We have included a Glossary on pages 107-110 to help students pronounce and define the words. Unlike a dictionary, the definitions in the Glossary are concise and written in context. Remember, we're teachers! Students will be exposed to these vocabulary words in the comprehension activities. They will also be tested on the vocabulary words four times throughout their study of *The Civil War*.

Students will be responsible for filling out and studying the vocabulary cards. You may want to have students bring in a small box for storing their vocabulary cards. We don't have to tell you that incorporating these words into your Reading and Spelling programs will save time and make the words more meaningful for students.

THE COPYRIGHT

Illustrations and cover design by Victoria J. Smith

ISBN 978-1-935255-06-2

OUR OTHER TITLES

COMPLETE STATE HISTORY PROGRAMS
Do American History!
Do Arizona!
Do California!
Do Colorado!
Do Nevada!
Do New Mexico!
Do Texas!
Do Washington!

LITERATURE STUDY GUIDES
Charlotte's Web
Cricket in Times Square
Enormous Egg
Sarah, Plain and Tall

AMERICAN HISTORY SERIES
New World Explorers
Spanish Explorers & Conquistadors
The Thirteen Original Colonies
Early American Government
The American Revolution
Slavery in America
Westward Expansion

U.S. REGION SERIES
The New England States
The Middle Atlantic States
The Great Lakes States
The Great Plains States
The Southeast States
The Southwest States
The Mountain States
The Pacific States

STATE HISTORY SERIES
Arizona Geography
Arizona Animals
Arizona History
Arizona Government & Economy
California Geography
California Animals
California History
California Government & Economy
Florida Geography
Florida Animals
Florida History
Florida Government & Economy
Texas Geography
Texas Animals
Texas History
Texas Government & Economy

TABLE OF CONTENTS

THE CIVIL WAR

VOCABULARY CARDS 1

CIVIL WAR K•W•L•H CHART 2

LESSON ONE: A NATION DIVIDED 5

A NATION DIVIDED READING COMPREHENSION 9

LETTER WRITING: BE PERSUASIVE! 10

VOCABULARY QUIZ PART I 14

LESSON TWO: THE CONFEDERATE ARMY 16

THE CONFEDERATE ARMY READING COMPREHENSION 18

LESSON THREE: THE UNION ARMY 19

THE UNION ARMY READING COMPREHENSION 22

CIVIL WAR VENN DIAGRAM: UNION VS. CONFEDERACY 23

COMPARE AND CONTRAST PARAGRAPH 25

VOCABULARY QUIZ PART II 26

LESSON FOUR: THE BATTLE OF BULL RUN 28

THE BATTLE OF BULL RUN READING COMPREHENSION 29

PRIMARY AND SECONDARY SOURCES: CONSIDER THE SOURCE 30

CIVIL WAR EXPERT'S JOURNAL 31

THE BATTLE OF BULL RUN JOURNAL ENTRY 32

LESSON FIVE: THE WESTERN THEATER 33

THE WESTERN THEATER READING COMPREHENSION 35

THE BATTLE OF WILSON'S CREEK JOURNAL ENTRY 36

THE BATTLES OF FORT HENRY AND FORT DONELSON JOURNAL ENTRY 37

THE BATTLE OF PEA RIDGE JOURNAL ENTRY 38

LESSON SIX: THE BATTLE OF SHILOH 39

THE BATTLE OF SHILOH READING COMPREHENSION 41

THE BATTLE OF SHILOH JOURNAL ENTRY 42

LESSON SEVEN: THE BATTLE FOR NEW ORLEANS 43

THE BATTLE FOR NEW ORLEANS READING COMPREHENSION 45

THE BATTLE FOR NEW ORLEANS DISCUSSION QUESTIONS 46

THE BATTLE FOR NEW ORLEANS JOURNAL ENTRY 47

THE WESTERN THEATER MAPPING 48

VOCABULARY QUIZ PART III 53

TABLE OF CONTENTS

THE CIVIL WAR (CONTINUED)

LESSON EIGHT: THE EASTERN THEATER 55

THE EASTERN THEATER READING COMPREHENSION 59

THE EASTERN THEATER DISCUSSION QUESTIONS 60

THE BATTLE OF YORKTOWN JOURNAL ENTRY 61

THE BATTLE OF FAIR OAKS JOURNAL ENTRY 62

THE BATTLE OF MALVERN HILL JOURNAL ENTRY 63

THE SECOND BATTLE OF BULL RUN JOURNAL ENTRY 64

LESSON NINE: INVASION OF THE NORTH 65

INVASION OF THE NORTH READING COMPREHENSION 68

THE BATTLE OF ANTIETAM JOURNAL ENTRY 69

THE EASTERN THEATER MAPPING 70

LESSON TEN: BATTLES OF 1863 75

BATTLES OF 1863 READING COMPREHENSION 79

THE BATTLE OF CHANCELLORSVILLE JOURNAL ENTRY.................................80

THE BATTLE OF GETTYSBURG JOURNAL ENTRY 81

THE BATTLE OF VICKSBURG JOURNAL ENTRY 82

LESSON ELEVEN: BATTLES OF 1864 83

BATTLES OF 1864 READING COMPREHENSION 86

THE BATTLES FOR ATLANTA JOURNAL ENTRY 87

SHERMAN'S MARCH TO THE SEA JOURNAL ENTRY 88

CIVIL WAR LETTER...89

LESSON TWELVE: THE END OF THE CIVIL WAR 93

THE END OF THE CIVIL WAR READING COMPREHENSION.............................95

THE END OF THE CIVIL WAR DISCUSSION QUESTIONS 96

THE DESTRUCTION OF RICHMOND JOURNAL ENTRY....................................97

SURRENDER AT APPOMATTOX JOURNAL ENTRY..98

CIVIL WAR EXPERT'S JOURNAL 99

LESSON THIRTEEN: RECONSTRUCTION..100

RECONSTRUCTION READING COMPREHENSION QUESTIONS............................103

CIVIL WAR K•W•L•H CHART DISCUSSION QUESTIONS 104

VOCABULARY QUIZ PART IV 105

GLOSSARY..107

ANSWER PAGES 111

BIBLIOGRAPHY...119

LESSONS at a GLANCE

1. Before reading A Nation Divided, students will:
   - complete Vocabulary Cards for *abandon, abolitionists, antislavery, candidate, Caribbean, coast, colonies, Confederate, Congress, constitution, convince, debate, economy, elected, governor, harbor, hostile, House of Representatives, inhumane, kidnapped, legislature, military, New World, outraged, plantation, profitable, resigned, Revolutionary War, secede, senator, societies, surrender, veteran, vowed, voyage. (pg. 1)*
   - complete first part of the Civil War K•W•L•H Chart. *(pps. 2-4)*

   After reading A Nation Divided *(pps. 5-8)*, students will:
   - answer A Nation Divided Reading Comprehension Questions. *(pg. 9)*
   - fill in any new information on the Civil War K•W•L•H Chart. *(pps. 2-4)*
   - use a graphic organizer to write a persuasive letter to Abraham Lincoln or Jefferson Davis. *(pps. 10-13)*
   - take a Vocabulary Quiz for the Civil War Part I. *(pps. 14-15)*

2. Before reading The Confederate Army, students will:
   - complete Vocabulary Cards for *admired, advantages, advisor, ammunition, borders, capital, confident, factories, invade, lieutenant, loyal, port, raids, superintendent, terrain. (pg. 1)*

   After reading The Confederate Army *(pps. 16-17)*, students will:
   - answer The Confederate Army Reading Comprehension Questions. *(pg. 18)*
   - fill in any new information on the Civil War K•W•L•H Chart. *(pps. 2-4)*

3. Before reading The Union Army, students will:
   - complete Vocabulary Cards for *blockade, canals, conflict, contrast, defeated, defending, expand, generals, major general, manufacturing, outranked, population, Potomac, promoted, raged, retired, strategy, tolerated. (pg. 1)*

   After reading The Union Army *(pps. 19-21)*, students will:
   - answer The Union Army Reading Comprehension Questions. *(pg. 22)*
   - fill in any new information on the Civil War K•W•L•H Chart. *(pps. 2-4)*
   - create a Venn Diagram comparing the Union and the Confederacy. *(pps. 23-24)*
   - use Venn Diagram to write a paragraph comparing the Union and Confederacy. *(pg. 25)*
   - take a Vocabulary Quiz for the Civil War Part II. *(pps. 26-27)*

LESSONS *at a* GLANCE

4. Before reading The Battle of Bull Run, students will:
   • complete a Vocabulary Card for *autobiography, biographies, historians, recruit.* *(pg. 1)*

   After reading The Battle of Bull Run *(pg. 28)*, students will:
   • answer The Battle of Bull Run Reading Comprehension Questions. *(pg. 29)*
   • fill in any new information on the Civil War K•W•L•H Chart. *(pps. 2-4)*
   • differentiate between primary and secondary sources. *(pg. 30)*
   • follow written directions for creating a Civil War Expert's Journal. *(pg. 31)*
   • research to create The Battle of Bull Run journal entry. *(pg. 32)*

5. Before reading The Western Theater, students will:
   • complete Vocabulary Cards for *brigadier general, gunboats, militia, muskets, outnumbered, rebel, steamboat.* *(pg. 1)*

   After reading The Western Theater *(pps. 33-34)*, students will:
   • answer The Western Theater Reading Comprehension Questions. *(pg. 35)*
   • fill in any new information on the Civil War K•W•L•H Chart. *(pps. 2-4)*
   • research to create The Battle of Wilson's Creek journal entry. *(pg. 36)*
   • research to create The Battles of Fort Henry and Fort Donelson journal entry. *(pg. 37)*
   • research to create The Battle of Pea Ridge journal entry. *(pg. 38)*

6. Before reading The Battle of Shiloh, students will:
   • complete Vocabulary Cards for *fleet, fortress, reinforcements, vessels.* *(pg. 1)*

   After reading The Battle of Shiloh *(pps. 39-40)*, students will:
   • answer The Battle of Shiloh Reading Comprehension Questions. *(pg. 41)*
   • fill in any new information on the Civil War K•W•L•H Chart. *(pps. 2-4)*
   • research to create The Battle of Shiloh journal entry. *(pg. 42)*

7. Before reading The Battle for New Orleans, students will:
- complete Vocabulary Cards for *bales, cavalry, fled, insulted, panicked, retreat, stronghold, transport.* *(pg. 1)*

After reading The Battle for New Orleans *(pps. 43-44)*, students will:
- answer The Battle for New Orleans Reading Comprehension Questions. *(pg. 45)*
- complete The Battle for New Orleans Discussion Questions. *(pg. 46)*
- fill in any new information on the Civil War K•W•L•H Chart. *(pps. 2-4)*
- research to create The Battle for New Orleans journal entry. *(pg. 47)*
- use a grid system to plot Western Theater Battles on a map. *(pps. 48-52)*
- take a Vocabulary Quiz for the Civil War Part III. *(pps. 53-54)*

8. Before reading The Eastern Theater, students will:
- complete Vocabulary Cards for *assault, demoted, former, peninsula, rally, telegraphed.* *(pg. 1)*

After reading The Eastern Theater *(pps. 55-58)*, students will:
- answer The Eastern Theater Reading Comprehension Questions. *(pg. 59)*
- complete The Eastern Theater Discussion Questions. *(pg. 60)*
- fill in any new information on the Civil War K•W•L•H Chart. *(pps. 2-4)*
- research to create The Battle of Yorktown journal entry. *(pg. 61)*
- research to create The Battle of Fair Oaks journal entry. *(pg. 62)*
- research to create The Battle of Malvern Hill journal entry. *(pg. 63)*
- research to create The Second Battle of Bull Run journal entry. *(pg. 64)*

9. Before reading Invasion of the North, students will:
- complete Vocabulary Cards for *conquered, Emancipation Proclamation, ford, harshly, mountainous, rebellion.* *(pg. 1)*

After reading Invasion of the North *(pps. 65-67)*, students will:
- answer Invasion of the North Reading Comprehension Questions. *(pg. 68)*
- fill in any new information on the Civil War K•W•L•H Chart. *(pps. 2-4)*
- research to create The Battle of Antietam journal entry. *(pg. 69)*
- use cardinal and intermediate directions to plot Eastern Theater Battles on a map. *(pps. 70-74)*

Lessons at a Glance

10. Before reading Battles of 1863, students will:
- complete Vocabulary Cards for *aggressive, civilians, dedication, founded.* *(pg. 1)*

After reading Battles of 1863 *(pps. 75-78)*, students will:
- answer Battles of 1863 Reading Comprehension Questions. *(pg. 79)*
- fill in any new information on the Civil War K•W•L•H Chart. *(pps. 2-4)*
- research to create The Battle of Chancellorsville journal entry. *(pg. 80)*
- research to create The Battle of Gettysburg journal entry. *(pg. 81)*
- research to create The Battle of Vicksburg journal entry. *(pg. 82)*

11. Before reading Battles of 1864, students will:
- complete Vocabulary Cards for *mill, plundered, riots, seaport, siege, trenches.* *(pg. 1)*

After reading Battles of 1864 *(pps. 83-85)*, students will:
- answer Battles of 1864 Reading Comprehension Questions. *(pg. 86)*
- fill in any new information on the Civil War K•W•L•H Chart. *(pps. 2-4)*
- research to create The Battles for Atlanta journal entry. *(pg. 87)*
- research to create Sherman's March to the Sea journal entry. *(pg. 88)*
- use a graphic organizer to write a Civil War letter to someone back home. *(pps. 89-92)*

12. Before reading The End of the Civil War, students will:
- complete a Vocabulary Card for *paroled.* *(pg. 1)*

After reading The End of the Civil War *(pps. 93-94)*, students will:
- answer The End of the Civil War Reading Comprehension Questions. *(pg. 95)*
- complete The End of the Civil War Discussion Questions. *(pg. 96)*
- fill in any new information on the Civil War K•W•L•H Chart. *(pps. 2-4)*
- research to create The Destruction of Richmond journal entry. *(pg. 97)*
- research to create Surrender at Appomattox journal entry. *(pg. 98)*
- follow written directions to finish Civil War Expert's Journal. *(pg. 99)*

LESSONS at a GLANCE

13. Before reading Reconstruction, students will:
- complete Vocabulary Cards for *accused, amendment, assassinated, citizens, ratify, Reconstruction, restricted.* *(pg. 1)*

After reading Reconstruction *(pps. 100-102)*, students will:
- answer Reconstruction Reading Comprehension Questions. *(pg. 103)*
- use Civil War K•W•L•H Chart to answer Discussion Questions. *(pg. 104)*
- take a Vocabulary Quiz for the Civil War Part IV. *(pps. 105-106)*

VOCABULARY CARD

word: _____

definition: _____

_____

_____

_____

VOCABULARY CARD

word: _____

definition: _____

_____

_____

_____

VOCABULARY CARD

word: _____

definition: _____

_____

_____

_____

THE Civil WAR

K·W·L·H CHART

Name _____

In 1861, the first shots of the Civil War were fired. In this activity you will use information from the next 13 lessons to learn about the Civil War. You will use the charts on the next two pages to record your information.

Before beginning your study of the Civil War, answer the three questions below.

1   Based on what you know about the Civil War *right now*, what is the most important thing you think people should know about the Civil War?

_____

_____

_____

2   Why is this the most important thing people should know about the Civil War?

_____

_____

_____

3   Do you think that learning new information will change what you think about the Civil War? Explain why.

_____

_____

_____

The Civil War © 2009
splashpublications.com

DIRECTIONS:

1. Use the "What I Know" column of the charts on the next two pages to list facts that you already know about the Civil War.

2. Use the "What I Want to Know" column of the charts to list six questions that you have about the Civil War.

3. As you study the Civil War, use the information you learn to answer your questions. Write your answers in the "What I Learned" column of the charts. At the end of your study, use books, encyclopedias, and the Internet to research any unanswered questions.

4. List the title of the lesson, book titles, encyclopedias, and website addresses that you used to find your information in the "How I Found Out" column of the charts.

WHAT I KNOW	WHAT I WANT TO KNOW	WHAT I LEARNED	HOW I FOUND OUT

The Civil War © 2009
splashpublications.com

WHAT I KNOW	WHAT I WANT TO KNOW	WHAT I LEARNED	HOW I FOUND OUT

A NATION DIVIDED

Slavery has been a part of American history since the early 1600s. Slave traders sailed across the Atlantic Ocean to the **coast** of Africa where they **kidnapped** innocent black men, women, and children. The slave traders crowded as many Africans as they could below the decks of their ships. After making the three month **voyage** to the **colonies** in the **New World**, the Africans were sold at auctions to Southern **plantation** owners who forced them into a life of slavery. This practice of buying and selling slaves continued for more than 200 years.

ABOLITIONISTS IN THE NORTH

By the end of the 1850s, the issue of slavery in the United States had become too big to ignore. Many Americans, especially in the Northern states, felt it was **inhumane** to claim ownership of another human being. The plantation owners in the South argued that they needed the slaves to help them on their huge tobacco and cotton plantations.

Southerners did everything they could to protect their **profitable** farming **economy** and cheap slave labor. Huge rewards were offered for runaway slaves. Laws were passed to punish **abolitionists** who helped slaves escape to freedom.

THE UNDERGROUND RAILROAD

Abolitionists in the North angered the slave owners by providing a path of freedom to slaves on what became known as the Underground Railroad.

Unlike a railroad with trains and tracks, the Underground Railroad was a system of homes throughout the United States, Canada, Mexico, and the **Caribbean** that hid runaway slaves on their way to freedom. The owners of the homes provided the runaway slaves with food and shelter. The slaves were then pointed in the direction of the next safe home along the "railroad."

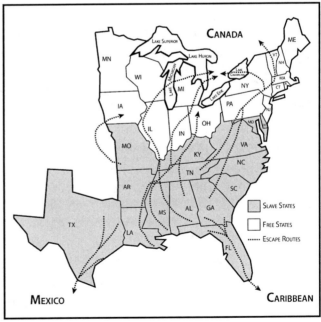

Abolitionists did not let the fear of punishment stop them from doing what they felt was right. Books and magazines that wrote about the cruel treatment of slaves were published. **Antislavery societies** were organized. Everyone feared that the United States was falling apart.

ABRAHAM LINCOLN

Abraham Lincoln was born in Kentucky on February 12, 1809. The Lincoln family owned a one-room log cabin on 348 acres of farmland that Abraham's father had purchased for $200. When Abraham was eight years old, the Lincoln family moved to Indiana. A year later, young Abraham's mother became ill and died.

Abraham was smart, even though he only went to school for 18 months. He loved to read, and at six foot four inches, he was unusually tall. He avoided fishing and hunting because he did not like killing animals, even for food.

Lincoln was a hard worker. He was very skilled with an ax, worked on a farm, built fences, and ran a store in Illinois. He was a captain in the Black Hawk War, where he fought against Native Americans in Illinois. In 1834, after being **elected** to the Illinois state **legislature**, Abraham Lincoln taught himself law. Three years later, he passed the test and became a lawyer.

In 1842, Abraham Lincoln married Mary Todd, the daughter of a wealthy slave owning family from Kentucky. They had four sons, but only one lived long enough to become an adult.

In 1846, Lincoln was elected to the **House of Representatives**. In 1858, he ran against Stephen A. Douglas for **senator**. He lost the election, but his views on slavery and his ability to **debate** made him very popular. In 1860, Abraham Lincoln became a **candidate** for president of the United States.

ABRAHAM LINCOLN

PRESIDENT ABRAHAM LINCOLN

Everyone hoped that choosing the right man for president would hold the nation together. Abraham Lincoln stood out as the country's favorite. Lincoln was not an abolitionist, but he did want to stop the spread of slavery into new territories. He promised to keep the United States from splitting into two pieces.

The Southern states were sure that a vote for Abraham Lincoln meant that slavery and their Southern way of life would end forever. The Southern states **vowed** to **secede** from the Union if Abraham Lincoln was elected as president of the United States.

On November 6, 1860, Abraham Lincoln became the sixteenth president of the United States. As promised, the Southern states made plans to separate from the Union. They wanted to form their own nation where slavery was legal and states could make their own decisions.

THE CONFEDERATE STATES OF AMERICA

South Carolina was the first state to secede from the Union. Within six weeks, Mississippi, Florida, Alabama, Georgia, and Louisiana withdrew as well. By early February 1861, the six states had formed a new government that it called the **Confederate** States of America. In all, 11 Southern states separated from the Union and joined the Confederacy.

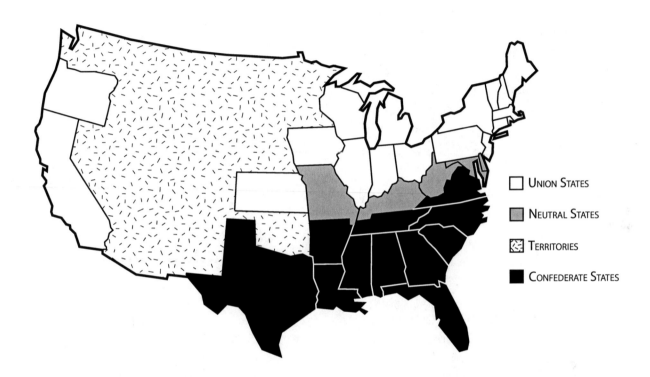

JEFFERSON DAVIS

Jefferson Davis was born in Kentucky, but he grew up in Mississippi. His father, Sam Davis, was a **veteran** of the **Revolutionary War**. At the age of 16, Jefferson Davis entered the United States **Military** Academy. He wasn't a very good student, but he graduated four years later.

After college, Jefferson Davis started his army career. For seven years, he helped the United States Army fight against **hostile** Native Americans. In 1835, he **resigned** from the United States Army. He married Sarah Taylor, and the two settled in Mississippi where they purchased black slaves and became cotton farmers. Sarah died of a fever after just three months of marriage.

In 1845, Jefferson Davis married Varina Howell. The couple had six children. For the next 15 years, Davis served as a member of **Congress**, fought in the Mexican War, tried to get elected as the **governor** of Mississippi, and was selected as secretary of war for the United States.

PRESIDENT OF THE CONFEDERACY

Jefferson Davis believed that states should make their own decisions about many important things. This included the issue of slavery. When the Confederate States of America was formed, Davis hoped to become the leader of the Confederate Army. Instead, he was elected as the president of the Confederacy.

The Confederate government wrote a new **constitution**, much like the one written by the United States. Slavery was protected in all Confederate states and any new territories that the Confederacy might gain.

The Confederate Constitution gave President Jefferson Davis permission to form a military force of 100,000 men and borrow 15 million dollars to help pay for a war.

President Lincoln was **outraged** that the Southern states had split the United States in half. Still, he promised Americans that the Union would not go to war unless the Confederacy attacked first.

JEFFERSON DAVIS

THE ATTACK ON FORT SUMTER

Fort Sumter was a Union fort in Charleston, South Carolina. In April 1861, President Lincoln sent ships to the Charleston **Harbor** loaded with supplies and troops for Fort Sumter.

President Jefferson Davis demanded that the Union **surrender** the fort because it was in Confederate territory. Union leader, Major Robert Anderson, refused to **abandon** Fort Sumter.

On April 12, 1861, Confederate troops fired cannonballs at Fort Sumter. These were the first shots of the Civil War. The Union troops returned fire. The battle for control of Fort Sumter continued for the next 34 hours.

After Fort Sumter was nearly destroyed and all of the supplies were gone, Major Anderson was forced to surrender. Neither side had lost a single man. The American flag was taken down and the Confederacy took control of Fort Sumter. The Union troops sailed to New York. The Civil War had officially begun.

Name _____

 ★ A NATION DIVIDED

Directions: Read each question carefully. Darken the circle for the correct answer.

1 Abolitionists in the North helped slaves escape to freedom. <u>Abolitionists</u> were –

   A against slavery

   B people who didn't want to get involved

   C in favor of slavery

   D Southern plantation owners

2 After reading about Abraham Lincoln, you get the idea that –

   F he loved animals

   G he was lazy

   H he was never married

   J he didn't know very much about the laws of our nation

3 Which phrase about Abraham Lincoln tells you that he was a smart man?

   A ...worked on a farm...

   B ...wealthy slave owning family from Kentucky...

   C ...taught himself law and became a lawyer...

   D ...fought against Native Americans in Illinois...

4 According to the information about Abraham Lincoln, how old was he when he became a candidate for president of the United States?

   F 33

   G 37

   H 49

   J 51

5 After Abraham Lincoln became president, which state seceded <u>first</u>?

   A Florida

   B South Carolina

   C Georgia

   D Mississippi

6 What can you learn by studying the Confederate and Union map?

   F There were more Confederate states than Union states.

   G The Confederate states were north of the Union states.

   H Most of the states were neutral.

   J There were more Union states than Confederate states.

7 Which event in Jefferson Davis's life took place <u>after</u> he got married?

   A He entered the United States Military Academy.

   B He resigned from the United States Army.

   C He fought in the Mexican War.

   D He fought against hostile Native Americans.

8 The first shots of the Civil War were fired by –

   F the Union

   G the Confederacy

   H Jefferson Davis

   J nobody really knows for sure

READING

Answers

1 Ⓐ Ⓑ Ⓒ Ⓓ   5 Ⓐ Ⓑ Ⓒ Ⓓ
2 Ⓕ Ⓖ Ⓗ Ⓙ   6 Ⓕ Ⓖ Ⓗ Ⓙ
3 Ⓐ Ⓑ Ⓒ Ⓓ   7 Ⓐ Ⓑ Ⓒ Ⓓ
4 Ⓕ Ⓖ Ⓗ Ⓙ   8 Ⓕ Ⓖ Ⓗ Ⓙ

LETTER WRITING
★ BE PERSUASIVE! ★

In 1861, the United States fell apart. Eleven Southern states seceded from the Union and formed the Confederate States of America.

In this activity, you will write a persuasive letter to Abraham Lincoln or Jefferson Davis. In a persuasive letter, the writer tries to **convince** another person to do something his or her way. Your persuasive letter should convince one of these leaders to find a way to end slavery and put the United States back together <u>without</u> going to war.

Directions: Write a persuasive letter to Abraham Lincoln or Jefferson Davis. Make sure your letter includes:

HEADING: Write your school name on the first line, your school address on the second line, and today's date on the third line.

GREETING: This is where you write the name of the person to whom you are writing. The Greeting usually starts with Dear _____ and always ends with a comma.

BODY: This is where you write your letter. The first sentence of the Body is always indented a few spaces.

CLOSING: This is where you end your letter. The Closing should match the type of letter you are writing. If the letter is to someone you don't know very well, you might use Sincerely or Best Regards. If the letter is to a friend, you might use Your Friend or Love. The Closing always ends with a comma.

SIGNATURE: This is the official end to your letter when you sign your name. The Signature is always in cursive.

- Before beginning your letter, organize your thoughts by answering the six questions on the next page.
- Write your rough draft on separate paper and have it edited.
- Write your final draft on the special paper provided by your teacher.
- When you are finished with your final draft, place it in the envelope that your teacher will give you. Properly address the envelope.
- Be prepared to read your letter aloud to the rest of the class!

★ ☆ ★ ☆ ★ ★ ☆ ★ ★ ☆ ★ ★ ☆ ★ ★ ☆ ★ ★ ☆ ★ ☆

1. Describe who you are and explain why you are writing this letter. _____

_____

_____

2. Give one reason why slavery should be ended.

_____

_____

_____

3. Give one reason why the United States should be put back together.

_____

_____

_____

4. Describe how you would like to see slavery ended and the United States put back together again without going to war.

_____

_____

_____

5. Describe how the United States would benefit from avoiding war.

_____

_____

_____

6. Describe how you plan to end your letter.

_____

_____

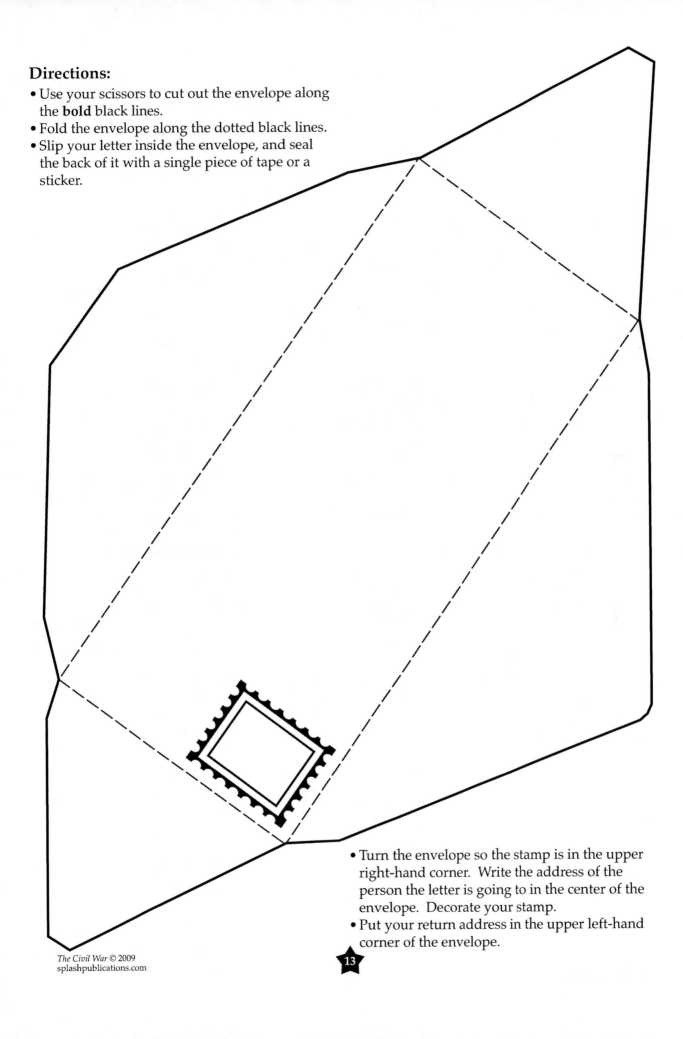

Directions:
- Use your scissors to cut out the envelope along the **bold** black lines.
- Fold the envelope along the dotted black lines.
- Slip your letter inside the envelope, and seal the back of it with a single piece of tape or a sticker.

- Turn the envelope so the stamp is in the upper right-hand corner. Write the address of the person the letter is going to in the center of the envelope. Decorate your stamp.
- Put your return address in the upper left-hand corner of the envelope.

☆ ★ ☆ ★★ Vocabulary Quiz ☆ ★ ☆ ★★

The Civil War
Part I

Directions: Match the vocabulary word on the left with its definition on the right. Put the letter for the definition on the blank next to the vocabulary word it matches. Use each word and definition only once.

1. _____ coast

2. _____ vowed

3. _____ colonies

4. _____ abandon

5. _____ societies

6. _____ abolitionists

7. _____ candidate

8. _____ veteran

9. _____ antislavery

10. _____ Confederate

11. _____ surrender

12. _____ constitution

13. _____ convince

14. _____ Congress

15. _____ House of Representatives

A.   to leave.

B.   settlements of people who are ruled by another country.

C.   a type of business that makes more money than it spends.

D.   the nation formed by the 11 Southern states during the Civil War.

E.   an arm of the Atlantic Ocean surrounded on the north and east by the West Indies, on the south by South America, and on the west by Central America.

F.   talk someone into doing something your way.

G.   selected leaders by voting for them.

H.   took someone without permission.

I.   someone who runs in an election contest.

J.   the way a city, state, or country makes money.

K.   a member of the Senate, one of two groups of people elected to Congress to make laws for our country.

L.   people who are part of the armed forces who may be asked to go to war.

M.   promised.

N.   withdraw from the Union.

O.   people who fought to end slavery.

16. _____ elected

17. _____ senator

18. _____ debate

19. _____ secede

20. _____ kidnapped

21. _____ economy

22. _____ governor

23. _____ resigned

24. _____ New World

25. _____ plantation

26. _____ harbor

27. _____ outraged

28. _____ profitable

29. _____ Revolutionary War

30. _____ inhumane

31. _____ hostile

32. _____ legislature

33. _____ voyage

34. _____ military

35. _____ Caribbean

P.   the branch of government that makes the laws.

Q.   against slavery.

R.   a very large farm in the South where crops of cotton and tobacco were grown and slave labor was usually used.

S.   to give up completely.

T.   very unfriendly.

U.   one of two groups of people elected to Congress to make laws for our country; the other part of Congress is the Senate.

V.   sheltered area of water deep enough to provide ships a place to anchor.

W. a person who has served time in the military.

X.   an area of land that borders water.

Y.   battle for independence between the English colonists in America and Great Britain.

Z.   journey that is usually made by water.

AA. a plan that outlines the duties of the government and guarantees the rights of the people.

BB. a term once used to describe the continents of North America and South America.

CC. quit.

DD. a discussion that gives arguments for and against a subject.

EE. angered beyond belief.

FF. groups of people who come together for a common cause.

GG. without kindness or compassion; unusually cruel.

HH. a person who is in charge of an area or group.

II.   the title given to the group of people in the Senate and House of Representatives who are elected to make laws for the United States.

THE CONFEDERATE ARMY

As soon as the first shots of the Civil War were fired, war fever seemed to sweep the country. Neither the Union nor the Confederacy was completely prepared for war, but each had **advantages** over the other. President Jefferson Davis immediately used the power given to him by the Confederate Constitution and asked for 100,000 volunteers to fight against the Union. Winning the first battle at Fort Sumter convinced many Southerners that the Civil War could be quickly won in a few months.

CONFEDERATE ADVANTAGES

The Confederate Army was very **confident** in its fighting ability. Southerners were used to being outside working and walking the **borders** of their huge plantations. They were also very comfortable carrying guns and riding horses. Northerners, on the other hand, lived in cities and worked in **factories**. They took trains from place to place.

The Confederacy also had Richmond, Virginia. Shortly after taking over Fort Sumter, the Confederacy moved its **capital** from Montgomery, Alabama, to the city of Richmond.

Richmond had railroad lines to the **port** cities of New Orleans in Louisiana, Savannah in Georgia, and Charleston in South Carolina. Richmond was also home to one of the largest gun making factories in the United States. The Confederacy would have all of the cannons and **ammunition** it could possibly need for the war effort.

The Confederacy decided early on that it could not successfully fight the Civil War in the North. It chose instead to wait for the Union Army to **invade** the South. Fighting the war on its own soil would be a huge advantage for the Confederate Army. The Confederate troops knew the **terrain** and the best hiding places. In addition, the Union did not have very good maps of the South.

The Union Army was limited and out of date. Its weapons were old and the Union didn't have enough cannons to fight a war. The Union Navy had 42 ships, but most of these were unfit for combat. Even the Union's commanders were outdated. The two most experienced officers in the Union Army were over the age of 70.

ROBERT E. LEE

When the Civil War started, over 300 officers resigned from the United States Army to join the Confederate Army. Leaders like Robert E. Lee were the Confederacy's biggest weapons.

Robert Edward Lee was born in Virginia on January 19, 1807. His father, Henry Lee, was known as "Light Horse Henry" during the Revolutionary War.

Robert grew up on his family's plantation in Virginia. He entered West Point Military Academy at the age of 18. His classmates **admired** him for his intelligence and leadership abilities. In 1829, Robert graduated with honors and became a **lieutenant** in the United States Army.

By the time the Civil War broke out, Robert E. Lee had already served the United States in many ways. He had been a leader in the Mexican War, the **superintendent** of West Point, and a lieutenant colonel in charge of protecting the settlers in Texas from Native American **raids**.

Although Lee was raised in Virginia, he was not in favor of slavery or separation from the United States. President Lincoln knew this and offered Robert E. Lee the job of commanding the Union Army. Lee turned down President Lincoln's offer and promised to stay **loyal** to Virginia.

ROBERT E. LEE

When Virginia seceded from the Union, Robert E. Lee kept his promise and resigned from the Union Army. He volunteered his services to the Confederacy. Robert E. Lee served first as an **advisor** to Confederate President Jefferson Davis. Later, he was **appointed** commander of the entire Confederate Army.

★═━★═ THE CONFEDERATE ARMY ═★━═★

Directions: Read each question carefully. Darken the circle for the correct answer.

1 **After reading the first paragraph about the Confederate Army, you learn that –**

   A the Union was more prepared than the Confederacy

   B President Jefferson Davis didn't have any power

   C the South believed the war would end quickly

   D the Confederacy lost the battle at Fort Sumter

2 **Which of the following was not one of the Confederate's advantages?**

   F The Confederate Army was confident in its fighting ability.

   G Southerners lived in cities and took trains from place to place.

   H The Confederacy was in control of Richmond, Virginia.

   J Southerners were used to being outside and riding horses.

3 **Which statement about the Union Army is false?**

   A The Union Army knew the terrain and the best places hiding places in the South.

   B The Union Army didn't have enough cannons to fight a war.

   C The Union Army didn't have very good maps of the South.

   D The two most experienced officers in the Union Army were over the age of 70.

4 **The Confederate Army decided to wait for the Union Army to invade. Invade means about the same thing as –**

   F attack

   G surrender

   H defend

   J kidnap

5 **After reading about Robert E. Lee, you get the idea that –**

   A he had never fought in a war before the Civil War

   B he was the first in his family to fight in a war

   C he was in favor of slavery

   D his loyalty forced him to turn down a job from the most important person in the Union

6 **Why did Robert E. Lee resign from the Union Army?**

   F He was angry with President Lincoln.

   G He promised to stay loyal to his state of Virginia.

   H He was too old to fight anymore.

   J He wanted to go back to school and become a lawyer.

READING

Answers

1 Ⓐ Ⓑ Ⓒ Ⓓ   4 Ⓕ Ⓖ Ⓗ Ⓙ

2 Ⓕ Ⓖ Ⓗ Ⓙ   5 Ⓐ Ⓑ Ⓒ Ⓓ

3 Ⓐ Ⓑ Ⓒ Ⓓ   6 Ⓕ Ⓖ Ⓗ Ⓙ

THE UNION ARMY

Within 48 hours of the Union's surrender at Fort Sumter, President Abraham Lincoln asked for 75,000 volunteers to help battle the Confederacy and bring the Union back together. President Lincoln and his supporters were confident that the Confederacy could be **defeated** in a short amount of time.

UNION ADVANTAGES

The North held most of the country's wealth, farm land, and railroad lines. The biggest banks with most of the nation's money were located in the North. The economy in the North included **manufacturing**, cattle, corn, wheat, and hogs. The Union Army had everything it needed to supply its soldiers.

The Union had twice as many states with a **population** of 22 million people. There were only 11 Confederate states with a total population of nine million. Three million of these people were black slaves. With all of its population and wealth, the Union could easily build a bigger and stronger army.

The North had more than 100,000 factories. Those factories made weapons for the Union Army. The farms in the North grew mostly food, while the huge plantations in the South grew a lot of cotton. The North was better prepared to feed its army. The North also had **canals** and 22,000 miles of railroad lines. These could be used to move soldiers and weapons from one battle to another.

THE UNION'S LEADERS

When the Civil War started, the Union Army included only 1,080 officers and 15,000 soldiers. Many of the best commanders in the United States Army lived in the South. As their states seceded from the Union, these men joined the Confederate Army. During the war, 142 of the Union's officers became **generals**. Though the Union Army was small at the beginning of the war, most of the Union's commanders had several years of military experience.

GEORGE B. MCCLELLAN

George Brinton McClellan was a young West Point graduate who had served in the Mexican War. During the first part of the Civil War, McClellan was **promoted** to **major general** and put in charge of training thousands of Union volunteers in Ohio, Indiana, Illinois, Pennsylvania, western Virginia, and Missouri.

Within a very short amount of time, McClellan **outranked** everyone except Lieutenant General Winfield Scott, the general in command of the entire Union Army.

After proving his leadership skills in two battles, President Lincoln immediately put General McClellan in charge of **defending** the Union's capital in Washington, D.C. General McClellan formed the Army of the **Potomac** with himself as commander. He defended the capital by building 48 forts with 480 guns and 7,200 soldiers.

General McClellan was in constant **conflict** with Lieutenant General Winfield Scott. The two disagreed on the **strategy** for winning the war. Lieutenant General Scott didn't believe that the Civil War would be a quick victory for the Union. He planned to set up a **blockade** of all Southern ports and keep the Confederacy from getting food or supplies to its soldiers.

General McClellan, on the other hand, wanted to **expand** the Union Army to 273,000 men and crush the Confederate Army in one short battle.

GENERAL IN CHIEF

On November 1, 1861, Lieutenant General Winfield Scott **retired** from the Union Army.

GEORGE B. MCCLELLAN

President Lincoln put General McClellan in charge of the entire Union Army. Unfortunately, President Lincoln quickly became angry with General McClellan's desire to build the Union Army and his slowness to actually attack. McClellan wouldn't share his war plans with his men or the officers serving under him.

In addition, General McClellan didn't believe that slaves should be set free. He viewed slaves as personal property and didn't think the government had any right to take away someone's personal property. McClellan promised the Confederacy that any slaves trying to escape would be returned to the South.

General McClellan's slowness to move and his views on slavery could not be **tolerated** by President Lincoln and the Union Army. Early in the war, President Lincoln removed McClellan from general in chief of the Union Army. McClellan was sent back to lead the Army of the Potomac.

ULYSSES S. GRANT

Ulysses Simpson Grant had been born in the Ohio River village of Point Pleasant. In 1843, at the age of 21, Grant graduated from West Point Military Academy. He had no interest in a military career. Instead, Ulysses wanted to teach mathematics to college students.

ULYSSES S. GRANT

The Mexican War spoiled Grant's plans of teaching. It also forced him to delay marriage to his sweetheart, Julia Dent. By the end of the war, Grant had proven himself as a brave soldier. He earned the rank of first lieutenant.

As soon as the Mexican War was over, Ulysses married Julia. Together they had four children. In 1854, Grant left the United States Army and settled with his young family in St. Louis, Missouri.

When the Civil War started, Ulysses S. Grant was almost 39 years old. He was against slavery and angry that the Southern states had seceded from the Union. Grant volunteered to fight for the Union Army.

Within the first year of the war, Grant earned rank as a general. He led his Union troops in several successful battles against the Confederacy.

General Grant was known as a tough talking leader who accepted nothing less than "unconditional and immediate surrender" from the enemy. During the summer of 1862, Grant was promoted to major general.

In 1864, Ulysses S. Grant took command of the entire Union Army. Under General Grant's leadership, the Union waged a total war on General Robert E. Lee and his Confederate troops. The Union destroyed everything in its path. This included homes, farms, crops, and railroads. During the final year of the Civil War, battles **raged** between the North and South. Thousands of lives were lost under General Grant's command.

Name _____

Directions: Read each question carefully. Darken the circle for the correct answer.

1   After reading the first paragraph about the Union Army, you learn that –

   A   the Confederacy surrendered Fort Sumter to the Union

   B   President Lincoln didn't think the Union needed any volunteers to fight the Confederacy

   C   nobody supported President Lincoln

   D   President Lincoln was sure the war would end quickly

2   Which of the following was <u>not</u> one of the Union's advantages?

   F   The Union had more people in it.

   G   The farms in the North grew mostly cotton.

   H   The North had 22,000 miles of railroad lines.

   J   There were more than 100,000 factories in the North.

3   Which statement about George B. McClellan is <u>true</u>?

   A   President Lincoln didn't trust General McClellan to defend the Union's capital.

   B   Before the Civil War, George McClellan had never fought in battle.

   C   General McClellan wanted to end the Civil War in one battle.

   D   McClellan always agreed with Lieutenant General Winfield Scott.

4   Which phrase about General McClellan describes why President Lincoln was not pleased with his abilities to lead the Union Army?

   F   ...graduated from West Point...

   G   ...slowness to actually attack...

   H   ...promoted to major general...

   J   ...defended the capital...

5   General McClellan was removed from general in chief of the Union Army for all of the following reasons <u>except</u> –

   A   McClellan spent too much time building an army an not enough time attacking the enemy

   B   McClellan didn't believe that slaves should be set free

   C   McClellan was not smart enough to lead the Union Army

   D   McClellan would not share his war plans with his men

6   Which event in Ulysses S. Grant's life happened <u>before</u> he got married?

   F   He took command of the entire Union Army.

   G   He fought in the Civil War.

   H   He was promoted to major general.

   J   He fought in the Mexican War.

READING

Answers

1   Ⓐ Ⓑ Ⓒ Ⓓ   4   Ⓕ Ⓖ Ⓗ Ⓙ
2   Ⓕ Ⓖ Ⓗ Ⓙ   5   Ⓐ Ⓑ Ⓒ Ⓓ
3   Ⓐ Ⓑ Ⓒ Ⓓ   6   Ⓕ Ⓖ Ⓗ Ⓙ

A Venn Diagram is a great tool to use when you want to create a graphic that shows how topics are different, yet alike at the same time. In a Venn Diagram, two or more large circles overlap in the middle. The differences between the chosen topics are written in the large outer areas of the circles. Things that the topics have in common are written where the circles overlap.

Look at the Venn Diagram below. There are two large circles that overlap to show how Abraham Lincoln and Jefferson Davis are both different and alike. In the large areas of the circles, the differences between Lincoln and Davis have been listed. The overlapping sections of the circles list the ways that Abraham Lincoln and Jefferson Davis are alike.

TOPIC: _____Abraham Lincoln_____   TOPIC: _____Jefferson Davis_____

Abraham Lincoln was very smart and loved to read. He was married to the same woman his entire life. The couple had four children.

Abraham Lincoln and Jefferson Davis were both presidents. Both men were born in Kentucky.

Jefferson Davis was not a very good student. His first wife died just three months after Jefferson married her. He married another woman. The couple had six children.

Directions: In this activity, you will use a Venn Diagram to compare and **contrast** the Union and the Confederacy so that you can write a paragraph. Use the information from the last few lessons as well as other books, encyclopedias, and the Internet to find the information for your Venn Diagram. Follow the example by listing the differences between the Union and the Confederacy in the large areas of the circles. Use the overlapping areas of the circles to list ways that the Union and the Confederacy were alike.

Name _____

Topic: _____ The Confederacy

The Confederacy's president was Jefferson Davis.

Both

the Union and the Confederacy wrote constitutions.

Topic: _____ The Union

The Union's president was Abraham Lincoln.

The Civil War © 2009
splashpublications.com

Directions: Use your Venn Diagram and a separate piece of paper to write a rough draft paragraph comparing and contrasting the Union and the Confederacy.

Your paragraph should include:

- a topic sentence clearly stating that you will be comparing and contrasting the Union and the Confederacy.
- two supporting sentences describing how the two were alike.
  Example: The Union and the Confederacy each wrote its own constitution outlining how laws would be made and enforced in their countries.
- two supporting sentences describing how the Union and the Confederacy were different.
  Example: The Union elected Abraham Lincoln as its president, while the Confederacy chose Jefferson Davis as its president.
- a closing sentence that "sums up" your paragraph.

Have someone edit your rough draft paragraph before writing your final draft in the space below. Attach extra paper if you need more space.

☆ ✦ ✩ ✦✦ VOCABULARY QUIZ ☆ ✦ ✩ ✦✦

THE CIVIL WAR
PART II

Directions: Match the vocabulary word on the left with its definition on the right. Put the letter for the definition on the blank next to the vocabulary word it matches. Use each word and definition only once.

1. _____ borders

2. _____ capital

3. _____ tolerated

4. _____ terrain

5. _____ admired

6. _____ blockade

7. _____ factories

8. _____ defeated

9. _____ strategy

10. _____ superintendent

11. _____ advantages

12. _____ canals

13. _____ major general

14. _____ manufacturing

15. _____ retired

16. _____ raids

17. _____ advisor

A.   won victory over.

B.   a person who helps make decisions and gives advice.

C.   well liked.

D.   a two-star officer in the United States Army who is one rank below a lieutenant general.

E.   a person who is in charge.

F.   man-made waterways for boats or for watering crops.

G.   a city or town located next to water with an area for loading and unloading ships.

H.   lies right next to something.

I.   grow larger.

J.   the city that serves as the center of government for the state or nation.

K.   a river that flows southeast from West Virginia to the Chesapeake Bay.

L.   protecting.

M.   put up with as long as possible.

N.   a struggle or disagreement.

18. _____ conflict

19. _____ population

20. _____ raged

21. _____ generals

22. _____ promoted

23. _____ loyal

24. _____ lieutenant

25. _____ invade

26. _____ confident

27. _____ ammunition

28. _____ Potomac

29. _____ outranked

30. _____ defending

31. _____ port

32. _____ expand

33. _____ contrast

O.   continued with great violence.

P.   enter an area and take it over by force.

Q.   bullets and explosive items used in war.

R.   the surface features of a piece of land.

S.   moved up in rank.

T.   making something from raw materials by hand or machinery.

U.   sudden attacks.

V.   to show the differences.

W.   buildings where large amounts of items are produced in the same way at the same time.

X.   favorable positions.

Y.   the lowest ranking officer in the United States Army.

Z.   without doubt.

AA. plan of attack.

BB. faithful.

CC. shutting off a place to keep people and supplies from coming in or going out.

DD. the number of people living in a place.

EE. had more authority than anyone else.

FF. left a job permanently to rest or try something else.

GG. army officers of one of the five highest ranks.

THE BATTLE OF BULL RUN

At the beginning of the Civil War, the Confederate capital was located in Montgomery, Alabama. A month later, it was moved to Richmond, Virginia. Many **historians** believe that moving the Confederate capital was a mistake. It placed the capital too close to the enemy. As a result, more than half of the 4,000 Civil War battles were fought on Virginia's soil. Many of these battles were fought in an effort to capture the Confederate capital.

THE BATTLE OF BULL RUN

On July 21, 1861, the first major battle of the Civil War was fought in Virginia. The Union's goal was to take control of the Confederacy's capital in Richmond. With 35,000 troops, the Union thought that the war would be over quickly. The well-trained Confederate soldiers met the Union troops at a small Virginia stream named Bull Run.

In the beginning of the battle, it looked as though General Irvin McDowell's Union soldiers would easily defeat Thomas Jackson's Confederate troops. By the end of the day, the Confederate soldiers had stood "like a stone wall." The Confederate troops pushed the Union Army back. From that day forward, Thomas Jackson was known as Thomas "Stonewall" Jackson.

The Battle of Bull Run cost many lives on both sides. The Confederacy lost 400 soldiers. The Union suffered 500 deaths. More than 3,500 Confederate and Union soldiers were wounded or missing. The Confederacy was sure that the victory at Bull Run would put an end to the war. Newspapers throughout the North wrote that it was best for our country to make peace with the South and give them what they want.

The Union refused to surrender the war to the Confederacy. Both sides realized that their hopes for a short, painless war were foolish. More troops were needed. Before the battle, the Union Congress called for 500,000 volunteers to serve for three years. After the loss at Bull Run, a new law added another 500,000 Union volunteers who were to serve the entire war, no matter how long it took. General George McClellan was put in charge of the new volunteers.

Confederate President Jefferson Davis asked for the Southern states to **recruit** 400,000 men who would serve for three years. In addition, volunteers who agreed to sign up for service again would receive a $50 bonus. President Davis put General Joseph E. Johnston in command of the Confederate's eastern troops.

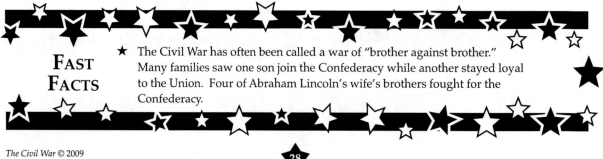

FAST FACTS

★ The Civil War has often been called a war of "brother against brother." Many families saw one son join the Confederacy while another stayed loyal to the Union. Four of Abraham Lincoln's wife's brothers fought for the Confederacy.

★—★ THE BATTLE OF BULL RUN ★—★

Directions: Read each question carefully. Darken the circle for the correct answer.

1 Why do many historians feel it was a mistake for the Confederacy to move its capital to Richmond, Virginia?

A Virginia was still part of the Union.

B It placed the Confederacy's capital too close to the enemy.

C There was no way to get food and supplies to the Confederate Army in Richmond.

D It placed the Confederacy's capital too far from the enemy.

2 Why did the Union Army choose to fight in Virginia?

F The Union wanted to take control of the Confederate capital and end the war.

G The Union wanted the weapons that were stored in Virginia.

H Virginia was the only Confederate state in the South.

J Most of the Union Army lived in Virginia.

3 The Battle of Bull Run was won by –

A the Union

B Abraham Lincoln

C General Irvin McDowell

D the Confederacy

4 After the Battle of Bull Run, Northern newspapers wrote that the Union should –

F try attacking again

G ask more people to join the Union Army

H make peace with the South and give them what they want

J replace General Irvin McDowell with someone else

5 After the Battle of Bull Run, new volunteers in the Union Army were expected to serve –

A two years

B six months

C until the end of the war

D five years

6 What did President Jefferson Davis do to convince volunteers to sign up for the Confederate Army again?

F He gave them money.

G He promised them better food.

H He promoted them to major generals.

J He told them they would only have to fight for two years.

7 The Battle of Bull Run made it clear to both the Union and Confederacy that –

A Abraham Lincoln was a poor leader

B the Civil War was not going to be over as quickly as everyone once thought

C nobody was going to stay loyal to the Confederacy

D President Jefferson Davis had a weak army

READING

Answers

1 Ⓐ Ⓑ Ⓒ Ⓓ   5 Ⓐ Ⓑ Ⓒ Ⓓ
2 Ⓕ Ⓖ Ⓗ Ⓙ   6 Ⓕ Ⓖ Ⓗ Ⓙ
3 Ⓐ Ⓑ Ⓒ Ⓓ   7 Ⓐ Ⓑ Ⓒ Ⓓ
4 Ⓕ Ⓖ Ⓗ Ⓙ

Think about the resources we use to learn about history. Reading books, seeing movies, looking at photographs, studying maps, searching the Internet, digging for bones, and holding pieces of pottery are some of the ways that we learn about the past.

There are two types of sources to help us learn about what happened in the past. Primary sources are recorded by people who were there at the time. If you have ever read a diary or an **autobiography**, then you were reading something that was written by the person who was actually recording the events and experiences as they were happening. Diaries and autobiographies are primary sources. Letters, interviews, photographs, original maps, bones, and pieces of pottery are other examples of primary sources because they give us "first-hand" knowledge of an event that took place in history.

Secondary sources are recorded by people after an event took place. Many books have been written about important historical events and people. A book written in 2005 about the life of a Virginia slave owner is a secondary source because the author wasn't actually there to interview the master and can't give any "first-hand" knowledge. Movies, **biographies,** newspaper stories, and encyclopedias are other examples of secondary sources because they give us "second-hand" knowledge of events that took place in history.

You have just finished studying about the Union and Confederate armies and the first battles of the Civil War.

In this activity, you will decide whether a source of information is a primary source or a secondary source. On the lines provided, put a "P" next to the primary sources and an "S" next to the secondary sources.

1. _____ The biography of Abraham Lincoln.

2. _____ The uniform of a Confederate soldier displayed in a Civil War museum.

3. _____ A story written about Jefferson Davis.

4. _____ Ulysses S. Grant's marriage certificate.

5. _____ A picture of Robert E. Lee taken in 1862.

6. _____ A letter written in 1864 from Abraham Lincoln to his wife Mary.

7. _____ A drawing of the Confederate flag.

CIVIL WAR
★ EXPERT'S JOURNAL ★

The Civil War was a series of several battles fought during a four year period. We know details about the Civil War and its many battles because of **primary sources** like diaries, journals, photographs, and letters. **Preserving** these important documents helps us to learn about the past.

In this activity, you will research Civil War battles to become an expert on the Civil War. You will use your information to create a *Civil War Expert's Journal* that includes important details about many important Civil War battles.

Directions:

1. During the next nine lessons, you will be learning about many important Civil War battles. After each lesson, your teacher will give you one or more pages for your *Civil War Expert's Journal*.

2. Use your information about the battles you have studied during the lesson and each of the *Expert's Journal* pages to fill in the required information about each Civil War battle. Spelling Counts!

3. Keep your journal pages in a safe place! After the last lesson, you will receive instructions about how to finish your *Civil War Expert's Journal*.

THE BATTLE OF BULL RUN

The Battle of Bull Run was the first major battle of the

Civil War fought in the state of _____

The Union's goal during the Battle of Bull Run was to

_____

_____

The Union soldiers were led by _____

_____

The Confederate troops were led by _____

_____

During the battle, Thomas Jackson received the

nickname _____

because_____

Victory for the Battle of Bull Run went to

_____

THOMAS JACKSON

One interesting fact about the Battle of Bull Run is_____

_____

_____

_____

_____

_____

_____

THE WESTERN THEATER

The Civil War was concentrated in two main areas, or theaters. The Eastern Theater included Maryland, Pennsylvania, and Virginia. The Western Theater stretched from eastern Kentucky and Tennessee down to the Gulf of Mexico and all the way to New Mexico.

The defeats at Fort Sumter and again at Bull Run worried President Lincoln. Since the beginning of the South's secession and the first shots of the Civil War, President Lincoln had been concerned that the border states would withdraw and join the Confederacy. Missouri, Kentucky, Maryland, and Delaware were four slave states that had not yet seceded. President Lincoln knew if these states joined the Confederacy, the Confederate Army would gain a huge advantage over the Union Army. If Maryland seceded, it would leave Washington, D.C. completely surrounded by Confederate states.

THE BATTLE OF WILSON'S CREEK

Missouri's governor, Claiborne Fox Jackson, wanted his state to secede. He refused to send troops to the Union Army. Montgomery Blair, a Missouri congressman, organized a group of Union volunteers that included a large number of Germans who were against slavery.

Blair's Union volunteers were placed under the command of Captain Nathaniel Lyon. By May 10, 1861, Captain Lyon and his troops had successfully captured a **rebel militia (muh•LIH•shuh)** in St. Louis and taken 20,000 **muskets**. For his success, Nathaniel Lyon was promoted to **brigadier (brih•guh•DEER) general**.

In August 1861, the Battle of Wilson's Creek found General Lyon and his Union troops **outnumbered** two to one by Major General Sterling Price and his Confederate soldiers. General Lyon divided his army and attacked the Confederates. Lyon was killed during the battle and his Union troops were defeated. More than 1,200 men died during the one day battle. The Confederacy gained control of the southern half of Missouri.

DEFEAT AT LEXINGTON

Sterling Price marched his Confederate troops north toward Lexington, Missouri. His 18,000 soldiers easily defeated 3,500 Union troops protecting a Union fort. Price's Confederate soldiers captured the fort, taking 3,000 rifles and 750 horses.

After the defeat at Lexington, Union General John C. Frémont freed all of the black slaves and ordered the killing of any Confederate soldiers captured by Union forces. President Lincoln was angered by General Frémont's bold move. Lincoln did not want to give Missouri a reason to secede from the Union and join the Confederacy. General Frémont was replaced with General Henry Wager, a West Point graduate whose nickname was "Old Brains."

THE BATTLES OF FORT HENRY AND FORT DONELSON

Fort Henry was a Confederate fort built on the banks of the Tennessee River. Just 12 miles away, the Confederacy built Fort Donelson on the Cumberland River. Together, these forts were the Confederacy's most important defense of the Mississippi River Valley. Taking control of these forts would cut the Confederacy in half and keep Kentucky under complete control of the Union.

In early February 1862, General Ulysses S. Grant and 15,000 Union soldiers traveled by **steamboat** up the Tennessee and Cumberland rivers. Seven Union **gunboats** followed them.

On February 6, the gunboats fired at Fort Henry. General Lloyd Tilghman and his Confederate soldiers quickly abandoned the fort.

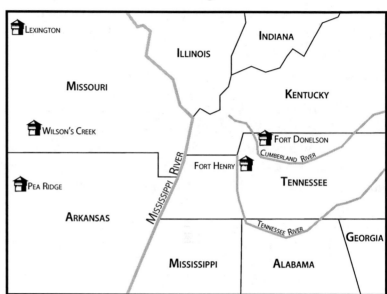

The Union's General Grant marched his men the short distance to Fort Donelson. The gunboats traveled up the Cumberland River to meet General Grant and his men a week later.

Trapped by Union forces, Confederate General John B. Floyd surrendered Fort Donelson. All 13,000 of General Floyd's Confederate soldiers were taken prisoner by the Union forces. The control of the Tennessee and Cumberland rivers belonged to the Union. These rivers would allow the Union to freely enter the South. Kentucky would remain part of the Union for the rest of the war. Ulysses S. Grant was promoted to major general after taking control of the forts.

THE BATTLE OF PEA RIDGE

While General Grant and his Union soldiers were capturing Fort Henry and Fort Donelson, the Confederate Army made plans to take complete control of Missouri. Major General Sterling Price and his 15,000 Confederate troops were joined by General Earl Van Dorn and 18,000 soldiers. On February 12, 1862, Major General Samuel R. Curtis and his Union soldiers attacked the Confederate troops near Springfield, Missouri. The attack sent the Confederate Army south into Arkansas.

In Arkansas, Confederate General Ben McCulloch and his Native American soldiers joined with General Van Dorn and Sterling Price. Together, they made their way back toward an area in northwest Arkansas known as Pea Ridge. General Curtis's Union troops were camping on top of Pea Ridge. They could clearly see the Confederate troops approaching.

On March 7, 1862, the Battle of Pea Ridge began with shots fired by General Curtis's Union troops. The Native American soldiers ran in different directions and Confederate General McCulloch was killed. Twenty four hours later, the battle was over. Though the Union lost twice as many men as the Confederacy, the victory gave the Union complete control of Missouri for the rest of the war.

THE WESTERN THEATER

Directions: Read each question carefully. Darken the circle for the correct answer.

1 The Western Theater of the Civil War stretched from eastern Kentucky and Tennessee down to the Gulf of Mexico. The Eastern Theater included all of the following states <u>except</u> –

A Maryland

B Kentucky

C Pennsylvania

D Virginia

2 Why was President Lincoln so concerned about the border states of Missouri, Kentucky, Maryland, and Delaware?

F They didn't have enough people in them to defend themselves against Confederate attacks.

G He was worried that their slaves would get hurt during the war.

H He was afraid that they would secede from the Union and join the Confederacy.

J He knew if the Union lost the Civil War, those four states wouldn't vote for him again.

3 After the Union's defeat at Lexington, what event angered President Lincoln?

A The Confederates captured a Union fort.

B Ulysses S. Grant resigned from the Union Army.

C General John C. Frémont freed all of the slaves captured by the Union.

D Missouri seceded from the Union.

4 After studying the map of forts on the Mississippi River, you learn that –

F Fort Donelson was south of the Cumberland River

G the Tennessee River runs through Arkansas

H Fort Henry was southwest of Fort Donelson

J the Mississippi River forms the southern border of Indiana.

5 Which commander led the Union troops in the capture of Fort Henry and Fort Donelson?

A General George McClellan

B General Nathaniel Lyon

C General John C. Frémont

D General Ulysses S. Grant

6 Why was winning the Battle of Pea Ridge so important to the Union?

F The Union took control of Missouri for the rest of the war.

G The Union didn't lose any men during the battle.

H The Confederacy lost twice as many men as the Union during the battle.

J Confederate General Robert E. Lee died during the battle.

Answers

READING

1 Ⓐ Ⓑ Ⓒ Ⓓ   4 Ⓕ Ⓖ Ⓗ Ⓙ

2 Ⓕ Ⓖ Ⓗ Ⓙ   5 Ⓐ Ⓑ Ⓒ Ⓓ

3 Ⓐ Ⓑ Ⓒ Ⓓ   6 Ⓕ Ⓖ Ⓗ Ⓙ

THE BATTLE OF WILSON'S CREEK

Missouri's governor, Claiborne Fox Jackson, wanted his state to _____

Governor Jackson refused to send troops to the _____

Montgomery Blair, a Missouri congressman, organized a group of Union volunteers that included _____

_____

Blair's Union volunteers were under the command of _____

In August 1861, the Battle of Wilson's Creek found General Lyon and his Union troops outnumbered by the Confederate soldiers. Outnumbered means

_____

During the Battle of Wilson's Creek, the Confederate soldiers were led by

_____

Victory for the Battle of Wilson's Creek went to _____

One interesting fact about the Battle of Wilson's Creek is _____

_____

_____

_____

_____

_____

_____

Map:
- LEXINGTON
- ILLINOIS
- INDIANA
- MISSOURI
- KENTUCKY
- WILSON'S CREEK
- FORT DONELSON
- CUMBERLAND RIVER
- FORT HENRY
- MISSISSIPPI RIVER
- PEA RIDGE
- TENNESSEE
- ARKANSAS
- TENNESSEE RIVER
- GEORGIA
- MISSISSIPPI
- ALABAMA

Fort Henry was a Confederate fort built on the banks of the _____ River. Fort Donelson was a Confederate fort built on the _____ River. If the Union could take control of these Confederate forts, _____

_____

_____

During the Battles of Fort Henry and Fort Donelson, the Union troops were led by _____

The Confederate troops were led by _____

and _____

Victory for the Battles of Fort Henry and Fort Donelson went to _____

One interesting fact about the Battles of Fort Henry and Fort Donelson is _____

_____

_____

_____

_____

THE BATTLE OF PEA RIDGE

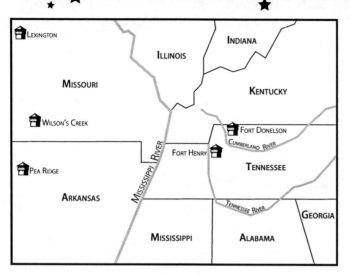

While General Grant and his Union troops were capturing Fort Henry and Fort Donelson, the Confederate Army made plans to take complete control of

_____

During the Battle of Pea Ridge,

the Union troops were led by _____

The Confederate troops were led by _____

and _____ and _____

The first shots of the Battle of Pea Ridge were fired by _____

Victory for the Battle of Pea Ridge went to _____

One interesting fact about the Battle of Pea Ridge is _____

_____

_____

_____

_____

_____

_____

_____

_____

THE BATTLE OF SHILOH

Since the beginning of 1862, the Union Army had successfully defeated the Confederacy in several important battles. The border states of Kentucky and Missouri were safely in the hands of the Union. The Union had control of the Tennessee and Cumberland rivers, giving it an opening into the South.

MOVING INTO THE SOUTH

Early in April 1862, General Ulysses S. Grant moved his army of 42,000 men to the western banks of the Tennessee River. He was waiting for General Don Carlos Buell to arrive with 25,000 Union **reinforcements**. General Grant had his men in the heart of Confederate territory and he knew they were in danger. Most of Grant's men were new soldiers who had never fought in battle before. If the Union Army was going to move south into Mississippi, it would need at least 70,000 men.

Just south of General Grant's troops, a Confederate force of 50,000 was protecting the railroad in Memphis, Tennessee. Confederate commander General Albert Johnston was planning to attack Grant before his reinforcements arrived. Johnston had already moved his men to within a few miles of Grant's force. The Union was on Confederate soil. General Johnston believed that his men could easily defeat the Union troops.

THE BATTLE OF SHILOH

On the morning of April 6, 1862, the attack began. More than 60 Confederate cannons blasted away at the Union Army. General Grant's men fought back, killing three out of every four men who came over the hill. General Johnston was shot several times and died. Still, the untrained Union troops defending the hill were pushed back, leaving their uneaten breakfasts for the Confederate troops to enjoy.

The first day of the Battle of Shiloh had been unlike any other since the beginning of the Civil War. Hundreds of bodies covered the battlefield. Thousands more were crying out in pain. Fortunately for Grant, General Buell and 25,000 fresh Union soldiers arrived during the night.

The next morning, the Confederate soldiers were surprised by how large the Union's army had grown. The Confederate troops were outnumbered and quickly surrendered.

Although General Grant won the Battle of Shiloh, he lost 3,500 men. More lives were lost in just two days than the total number of lives lost in the Revolutionary War, the War of 1812, and the Mexican War.

THE MISSISSIPPI RIVER

During the remainder of 1862, the Union continued on to its goal of controlling the Mississippi River. Taking control of the Mississippi River and the cities that bordered it were important to winning the war.

In the spring of 1862, a **fleet** of more than 100 Union river **vessels** and gunboats successfully captured Island Number 10. Island Number 10 was a Confederate **fortress** on the Mississippi River with about 50 cannons. Over the next few months, other Confederate forts along the Mississippi River surrendered to the Union.

On May 10, 1862, Confederate forces were defeated at Fort Pillow. A few weeks later, the Tennessee city of Memphis was captured during a battle that lasted just over an hour. The Union tightened its grip on the Mississippi River.

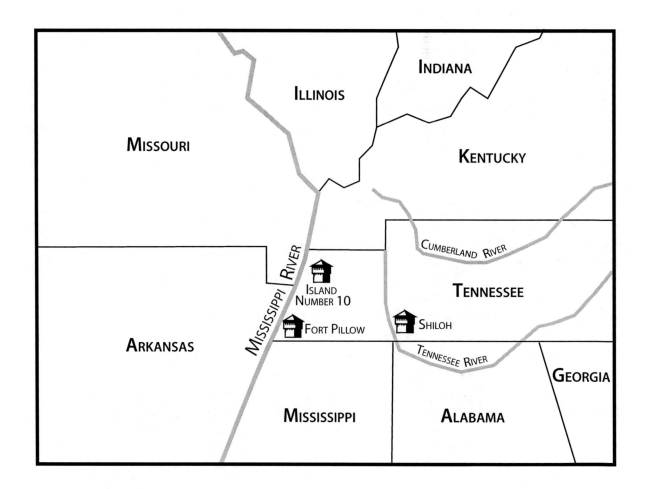

Name _____

THE BATTLE OF SHILOH

Directions: Read each question carefully. Darken the circle for the correct answer.

1   Since the beginning of 1862, the Union Army had successfully done all of the following except –

A   gained control of Kentucky

B   taken control of the Confederate capital

C   gained control of Missouri

D   taken control of the Tennessee and Cumberland rivers

2   Why was General Grant worried when he moved his men to the western banks of the Tennessee River?

F   He knew his men couldn't swim across the river.

G   It was getting dark and he was afraid that his men wouldn't be able to see where they were going.

H   He was in the middle of Confederate territory and he was afraid for the safety of his men.

J   He had too many men in a very small area.

3   On the second day of the Battle of Shiloh, why did the Confederate Army surrender so quickly?

A   They realized they were outnumbered.

B   Their leader had been killed.

C   They ran out of ammunition.

D   Their cannons weren't firing properly.

4   In the spring of 1862, a fleet of 100 Union vessels captured a Confederate fort. A fleet is a –

F   commander

G   large group

H   single ship

J   body of water

5   What can you learn by studying the map of forts on the Mississippi River?

A   Island Number 10 is west of the Mississippi River.

B   The Battle of Shiloh took place north of the Cumberland River.

C   The Tennessee River is west of Fort Pillow.

D   The Battle of Shiloh took place east of the Mississippi River.

6   Which of the following is an example of a primary source?

F   A reenactment of the Battle of Shiloh.

G   A story about General Ulysses S. Grant.

H   A photograph of Fort Pillow.

J   A book written in 2004 about capturing the Confederate forts on the Mississippi River.

READING

Answers

1   Ⓐ Ⓑ Ⓒ Ⓓ   4   Ⓕ Ⓖ Ⓗ Ⓙ
2   Ⓕ Ⓖ Ⓗ Ⓙ   5   Ⓐ Ⓑ Ⓒ Ⓓ
3   Ⓐ Ⓑ Ⓒ Ⓓ   6   Ⓕ Ⓖ Ⓗ Ⓙ

The Civil War © 2009
splashpublications.com

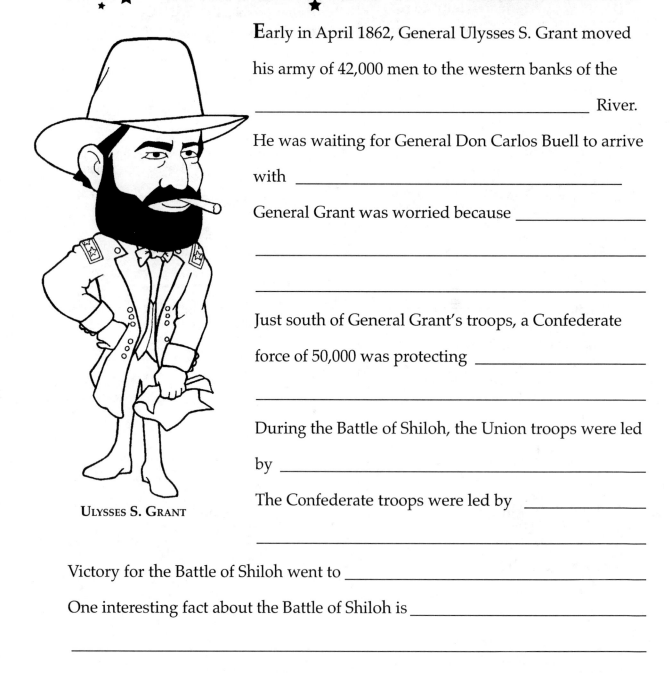

ULYSSES S. GRANT

Early in April 1862, General Ulysses S. Grant moved

his army of 42,000 men to the western banks of the

_____ River.

He was waiting for General Don Carlos Buell to arrive

with _____

General Grant was worried because _____

_____

_____

Just south of General Grant's troops, a Confederate

force of 50,000 was protecting _____

_____

During the Battle of Shiloh, the Union troops were led

by _____

The Confederate troops were led by _____

_____

Victory for the Battle of Shiloh went to _____

One interesting fact about the Battle of Shiloh is _____

_____

_____

_____

_____

★THE BATTLE FOR NEW ORLEANS★

New Orleans was the largest of the Confederate cities. It was located at the mouth of the Mississippi River. The Confederacy used this port to ship and receive important products to and from other states in the South and the Caribbean. As the Union gained control of the Mississippi River, the Confederacy was cut off from New Orleans, its most important city. The Union knew that it had to take complete control of New Orleans and its valuable port.

FORT JACKSON AND FORT ST. PHILIP

More than 10,000 Confederate troops protected the city of New Orleans. Fort Jackson and Fort St. Philip provided protection from Union ships entering from the Gulf of Mexico. Fort Jackson was a star-shaped stone fort with 74 cannons. Fort St. Philip was also built of stone and held 52 guns. More than 700 Confederate soldiers were stationed at the forts.

A long length of chain stretched into the Mississippi River, guarding the entrance to the forts. In addition, rebel gunboats were ready to fire upon any unwanted visitors. Fortunately, back in 1861, the Union had captured Ship Island located just off the coast of Mississippi in the Gulf of Mexico. The Union could use its position on Ship Island to plan its attack on New Orleans.

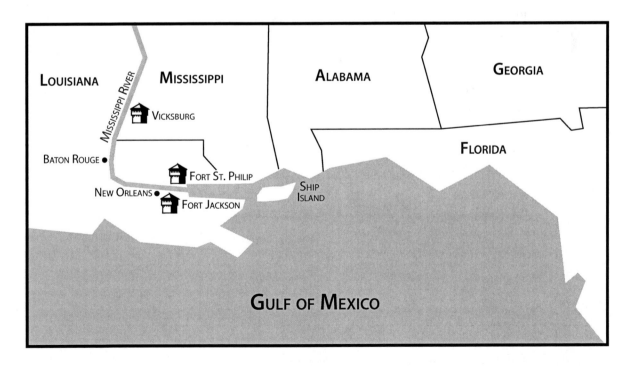

David G. Farragut

Officer David G. Farragut was chosen to capture New Orleans. Farragut had entered the United States Navy when he was just nine years old. At 12, he fought in the War of 1812, where he was given command of a ship. Over the next 50 years, Farragut proved his loyalty to the United States. At the beginning of the Civil War, he came out of retirement to once again join the Navy and help bring the United States back together.

Capturing Fort Jackson and Fort St. Philip

Officer Farragut's men left from Ship Island in the Gulf of Mexico. They sailed west toward the Mississippi River in 20 wooden ships. For more than a week, they fired 16,000 cannonballs at Fort Jackson and Fort St. Philip. Though Fort Jackson caught on fire, neither fort was destroyed.

The Union's ships were able to damage the chain that stretched into the Mississippi River. The Union fleet sailed toward New Orleans. For more than an hour, Union and Confederate ships fired at each other. Rebel soldiers guarding the forts fired cannonballs at the Union's wooden ships, catching at least one on fire. The Union sank several Confederate ships, forcing the rebels to surrender.

The City of New Orleans

In the city of New Orleans, residents **panicked**. Confederate commander General Mansfield Lovell knew that his 3,000 untrained volunteers with shotguns were no match for the Union's cannonballs. He removed his men from New Orleans, leaving the city with no way to defend itself.

Confederates set fire to anything of value, including 15,000 **bales** of cotton, boats, and naval ships. Rice, molasses, and sugar were thrown into the river. The citizens withdrew four million dollars from the city's banks and **fled**.

Twenty thousand Union troops were sent to take control of the city. Confederate citizens who remained in New Orleans refused to give in to the Union's demands. Union soldiers were **insulted** and spit upon. American flags were destroyed.

David G. Farragut

Over the next few months, the Union used its position in New Orleans to take control of Baton (BAT•un) Rouge (ROOZH), Louisiana. This left the Mississippi city of Vicksburg as the last major Confederate **stronghold** on the southern end of the Mississippi River.

Name _____

Directions: Read each question carefully. Darken the circle for the correct answer.

1   **New Orleans was important to the Confederacy because –**

  A   it had the most railroad tracks of any Confederate city

  B   it grew more cotton than any other Confederate city

  C   it was a port for shipping and receiving important products

  D   there were more slaves in New Orleans than in any other Confederate city

2   **Which forts protected the entrance to the city of New Orleans?**

  F   Vicksburg and Baton Rouge

  G   Fort St. Philip and Ship Island

  H   Fort Jackson and Mississippi Fort

  J   Fort St. Philip and Fort Jackson

3   **After studying the map on the first page, you learn that –**

  A   Ship Island is northeast of Fort Jackson

  B   the Gulf of Mexico is north of New Orleans

  C   Florida is east of Georgia

  D   Vicksburg is northwest of Fort St. Philip

4   **According to the map on the first page, Mississippi is –**

  F   north of Louisiana

  G   south of Louisiana

  H   west of Louisiana

  J   east of Louisiana

5   **Which statement about David G. Farragut is true?**

  A   David Farragut was born after the War of 1812.

  B   David Farragut refused to fight in the Civil War.

  C   David Farragut wasn't even a teenager when he joined the United States Navy.

  D   The United States did not trust David Farragut to capture New Orleans.

6   **After reading about David Farragut's capture of Fort Jackson and Fort St. Philip, you get the idea that –**

  F   it only took a few cannonballs to capture the forts

  G   both forts were completely destroyed during the battle

  H   the Confederates guarding the forts never fired cannons of their own

  J   in the end, the Confederates were forced to surrender

7   **What happened when David Farragut and his men reached the city of New Orleans?**

  A   The Confederate soldiers abandoned the city.

  B   The Confederates loaded their cannons and fought back.

  C   Everyone in the city stayed calm.

  D   The residents welcomed the Union soldiers.

READING

Answers

1 Ⓐ Ⓑ Ⓒ Ⓓ   5 Ⓐ Ⓑ Ⓒ Ⓓ
2 Ⓕ Ⓖ Ⓗ Ⓙ   6 Ⓕ Ⓖ Ⓗ Ⓙ
3 Ⓐ Ⓑ Ⓒ Ⓓ   7 Ⓐ Ⓑ Ⓒ Ⓓ
4 Ⓕ Ⓖ Ⓗ Ⓙ

LET'S TALK ABOUT IT

THE BATTLE FOR NEW ORLEANS

The Battle for New Orleans ended with a victory for the Union. Read the questions below about the Battle for New Orleans. Write your answers on the lines provided. Attach a separate piece of paper if you need more room. Be ready to discuss some of your answers.

• **Control of Fort Jackson and Fort St. Philip were very important to the Union.**

Based on what you have learned, explain why taking control of these forts was so important to the Union.

_____

_____

_____

If the Union hadn't been able to take control of Fort Jackson and Fort St. Philip, what do you think would have happened next?

_____

_____

_____

• **After the Union captured New Orleans, the Confederates set fire to the city and withdrew all of their money from the bank.**

Why do you think the citizens of New Orleans destroyed their own city and drained the bank of money?

_____

_____

_____

_____

★ THE BATTLE FOR NEW ORLEANS ★

New Orleans was the largest of the Confederate cities.

The Confederacy used New Orleans to _____

_____

As the Union took control of the Mississippi River, the

Confederacy _____

_____

Fort Jackson and Fort Philip were controlled by the

_____

During the Battle for New Orleans, the Union troops

were led by _____

Confederate volunteers in New Orleans were led by

_____

Victory for the Battle for New Orleans went to

_____

DAVID G. FARRAGUT

One interesting fact about the Battle for New Orleans is_____

_____

_____

_____

_____

_____

_____

Using a **grid system** helps you locate places in the world. A **grid system** is made up of lines that come together to form squares. The squares divide a map into smaller pieces, making it easier to find important places. Learning how to use a **grid system** is easy, and will teach you an important location skill.

Example: The Battle of Wilson's Creek was the first major Civil War battle to take place west of the Mississippi River. The Confederates won the battle and took the life of Union General Nathaniel Lyon as well. The Battle of Wilson's Creek was fought at (4,18).

Locate the Battle of Wilson's Creek at (4,18), by putting your finger on the number 1 at the bottom of the grid. Slide **over** to 4 and **up** to 18. The Battle of Wilson's Creek was fought in the square created where these two numbers come together. This square has been colored in on the map below.

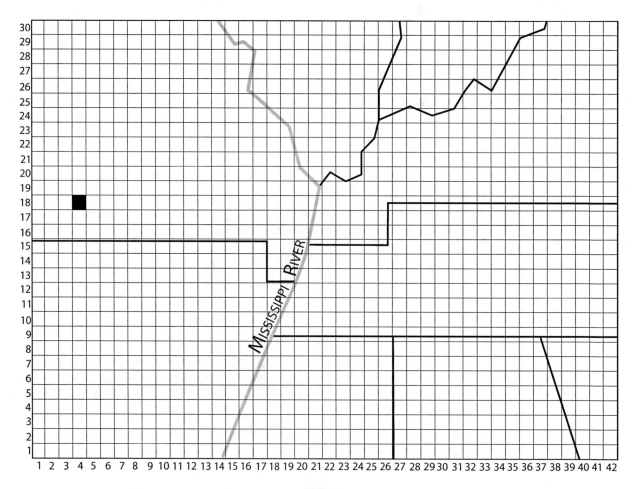

Directions: In this activity, you will use a grid system to locate important Western Theater battles during the first two years of the Civil War.

1. Follow the example for locating each Western Theater battle by going **over** and **up**. If a battle is located at (4,18), go **over** to 4 and **up** to 18.

2. When you locate a battle on the grid, color in the square with a coloring pencil. If the battle was won by the Confederacy, color in the square with a red coloring pencil. If the battle was won by the Union, color in the square with the blue coloring pencil.

3. When you are finished, ask your teacher to pull down the classroom map of the United States. Neatly label each state on your map with its correct name. Spelling counts!

1. The Battle of Barbourville was fought on September 19, 1861. In an effort to take control of this important border state, 800 Confederate troops attacked just 300 Union troops. The Confederate victory cost the Union one man, while the Confederates lost seven men. The Battle of Barbourville as fought at (41,19).

2. The Battle of Lexington was fought on September 20, 1861. The Union fort was being guarded by 3,500 Union soldiers. 18,000 Confederate troops surrounded the fort and forced the Union to surrender. The Battle of Lexington was fought at (2,29).

3. The Battle of Camp Wildcat was fought on October 21, 1861. Before the battle broke out, 7,000 Union troops hid alongside a road that the Confederate soldiers would have to cross. The fierce battle forced the Confederates to **retreat**, giving the Union a much needed victory. The Battle of Camp Wildcat was fought at (40,20).

4. The Battle of Mill Springs was fought on January 19, 1862. Though it was a small battle, it was one of the largest in this state. The Union won the battle, losing 39 men. The Confederates lost 125 men during the battle. More than 600 Union and Confederate soldiers were wounded or missing when the battle ended. The Battle of Mill Springs was fought at (38,20).

5.   The First Battle of Corinth was fought from April 29 to June 10, 1862. Union troops surrounded the town and prepared to attack. The Confederates saved themselves by sneaking onto a train that the Union thought was bringing Confederate reinforcements. When the Union attacked, they found the town empty. The Union declared victory. The First Battle of Corinth was fought at (25,8).

6.   The Battle of Fort Henry was fought on February 6, 1862. Gunfire from the Union Army and Navy at the same time panicked the Confederate commander, who quickly surrendered Fort Henry to the Union. The Battle of Fort Henry was fought at (27,16).

7.   The Battle of Fort Donelson was fought on February 12, 1862. Union gunboats traveled up the Tennessee and Cumberland rivers, firing at Fort Donelson. The Confederate troops guarding the fort quickly surrendered, giving the Union the victory. All 13,000 Confederate soldiers were taken prisoner after the battle. The Battle of Fort Donelson was fought at (29,17).

8.   The Battle of Shiloh was fought on April 6 and April 7, 1862. After a successful first day of battle for the Confederates, Union reinforcements arrived and outnumbered the Confederate troops. The Union declared victory. More men lost their lives during the two day battle than all of the soldiers who died in the Revolutionary War, the War of 1812, and the Mexican War. The Battle of Shiloh was fought at (27,10).

9.   The Battle of Island Number 10 was fought in the spring of 1862. The 50 Confederate cannons on the island were no match for the fleet of more than 100 Union river vessels and gunboats. The Union successfully captured Island Number 10. The Battle of Island Number 10 was fought at (21,14).

10.   The First Battle of Chattanooga was fought on June 7 and June 8, 1862. Though it was a minor battle, almost 100 Union and Confederate soldiers lost their lives. The Union victory sent a clear message to the Confederates: the Union soldiers were prepared to fight. The First Battle of Chattanooga was fought at (36,11).

11.   The Battle of Murfreesboro was fought on July 13, 1862. During the early part of July, the Confederate **cavalry** rode through the area raiding Union forts. By the 13th of July, 1,400 Confederate soldiers had captured Murfreesboro, an important Union supply center on the Nashville and Chattanooga railroads. The Battle of Murfreesboro was fought at (33,14).

12. The Battle of Richmond was fought on August 29 and August 30, 1862. After two days of battle, the Confederates forced the Union troops to surrender. More than 4,000 Union soldiers were captured by the Confederates. The Battle of Richmond was fought at (38,25).

13. The Battle of Munfordville was fought from September 14 to September 17, 1862. The victory during the three day battle allowed the Confederates to control the region and damage Union supply lines. The Battle of Munfordville was fought at (33,20).

14. The Battle of Luka was fought on September 19, 1862. The Union won the battle, stopping the Confederates from moving any further into this state. The Battle of Luka was fought at (26,8).

15. The Battle of Hatchie's Bridge was fought on October 5, 1862. Though the Union won the battle, the Union commanders missed the chance to capture a large group of Confederate soldiers. The Battle of Hatchie's Bridge was fought at (21,9).

16. The Battle of Perryville was fought on October 8, 1862. Remembered as one of the bloodiest battles of the Civil War, the Battle of Perryville was a Confederate victory. More than 1,300 men lost their lives during the one day battle. The Battle of Perryville was fought at (32,23).

17. The Battle of Hartsville was fought on December 7, 1862. Though the Union outnumbered the Confederate troops two to one, the Confederates forced the Union to surrender. During the battle, the Confederates took almost 2,000 Union soldiers as prisoners. The Battle of Hartsville was fought at (32,16).

18. The Battle of Jackson was fought on December 19, 1862. The goal of the Confederate Army was to destroy the Mobile and Ohio Railroad so the Union wouldn't be able to **transport** men or supplies to their battles. The Confederates were successful and claimed victory for the battle. The Battle of Jackson was fought at (22,10).

19. The Battle of Chickasaw Bayou was fought from December 26 to December 29, 1862. The Union, with more than 30,000 men, tried to take control of Vicksburg. Vicksburg was an important Confederate fort on the Mississippi River. The Confederates only had 13,000 men, but they successfully defended Vicksburg and claimed victory for the battle. The Battle of Chickasaw Bayou was fought at (16,2).

Name _____

The Western Theater 1861-1862

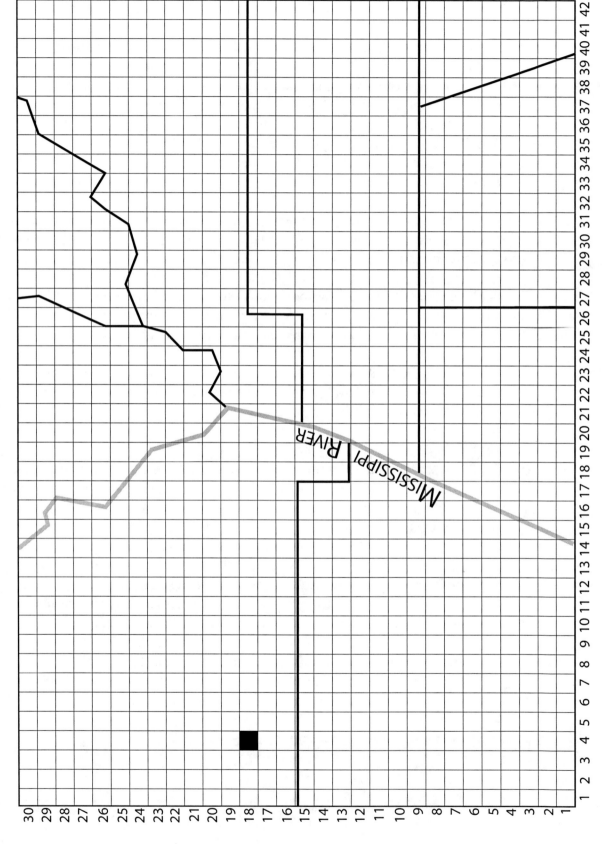

MISSISSIPPI RIVER

The Civil War © 2009
splashpublications.com

Name _____

Directions: Match the vocabulary word on the left with its definition on the right. Put the letter for the definition on the blank next to the vocabulary word it matches. Use each word and definition only once.

1. _____ steamboat

2. _____ recruit

3. _____ autobiography

4. _____ militia

5. _____ fleet

6. _____ bales

7. _____ brigadier general

8. _____ rebel

9. _____ biographies

10. _____ fortress

11. _____ transport

12. _____ historians

13. _____ gunboats

14. _____ outnumbered

A. a person who fights against the government of his or her own country.

B. the story of your life written by you.

C. more soldiers sent to help win a battle.

D. large group of ships.

E. to back away.

F. large boats.

G. treated someone badly by calling them names.

H. to find people who are willing to join a military force.

I. move products or people from one place to another.

J. had more people on one side than the other.

K. a well protected area.

L. a group of forts guarding a city or town.

M. stories of a person's life written by someone else.

15. _____ reinforcements

16. _____ cavalry

17. _____ vessels

18. _____ fled

19. _____ muskets

20. _____ insulted

21. _____ panicked

22. _____ retreat

23. _____ stronghold

N. heavy guns used by soldiers.

O. people who study history.

P. a group of people having some military training who are called upon only in emergencies.

Q. ran away from danger.

R. small ships equipped with guns.

S. became suddenly filled with fear.

T. a boat that is powered by a steam engine.

U. tightly wrapped packages of cotton or hay.

V. military troops riding on horseback.

W. a one-star officer in the United States Army who is one rank below a major general.

THE EASTERN THEATER

The summer of 1862 ended with Union victories in Kentucky, Louisiana, Missouri, and Tennessee. The important city of New Orleans had been captured by the Union and most of the forts along the Mississippi River were in the hands of Union forces. It had been a pretty successful year for the Union in the Western Theater. The Eastern Theater, however, did not result in as many early victories as President Lincoln had hoped.

THE PENINSULA CAMPAIGN

Since the beginning of the Civil War, the Union's goal was to capture the Confederacy's capital in Richmond, Virginia. The Battle of Bull Run was the Union's first attempt to take control of Richmond. It had ended badly for the Union. Thomas "Stonewall" Jackson's Confederate troops pushed the Union soldiers back, forcing them to surrender.

In March 1862, the Union's General George McClellan and his troops floated down the Chesapeake Bay from Washington to Fort Monroe on the Virginia **Peninsula**. Known as the Peninsula Campaign, McClellan's simple plan was to march up the peninsula straight toward the Confederate capital in Richmond.

After reaching the Virginia Peninsula, General McClellan realized that he was in trouble. The maps that McClellan had were incorrect. Instead of finding roads shown on the maps, McClellan's men found muddy paths and rivers that could not be crossed. It took weeks for McClellan's 120,000 men, 15,000 horses, and 1,100 wagons loaded with supplies to reach Yorktown.

THE BATTLE OF YORKTOWN

There were only 15,000 Confederate soldiers guarding Yorktown. Confederate commander, General John Magruder, tricked General McClellan into believing there were thousands more. General Magruder ordered his men to repeatedly fire their cannons and guns. He also instructed the bands to play first at one site and then quickly move to another and play again. This would make the Union troops think they were outnumbered.

General McClellan was fooled by Magruder's plan. Instead of attacking, McClellan **telegraphed** Washington and told President Lincoln that the Confederacy had more than 100,000 soldiers protecting the Confederate capital. McClellan's refusal to attack gave the Confederate Army plenty of time to move more troops in place to protect Richmond. The Union failed to take control of the Confederate capital and perhaps bring an early end to the war.

THE BATTLE OF FAIR OAKS

A month later, General McClellan was ready to try again. He marched toward Richmond, ordering his men to attack in Williamsburg, Virginia. More than 4,000 Union and Confederate soldiers lost their lives during the battle.

As the Union troops continued on toward the capital, Confederate commander General Joe Johnston circled his troops around Richmond. McClellan split his troops in two, sending part of them north to join up with 40,000 Union forces that were being sent from Washington. The remaining Union troops were sent south toward the Confederate capital.

Five miles from Richmond, General McClellan panicked. He realized that the 40,000 troops from Washington never arrived. President Lincoln kept them in Washington to guard the Union's capital.

CIVIL WAR CANNON

On May 31, 1862, General Johnston and his Confederate force of 31,000 men attacked General McClellan's army of 19,000. During the two day battle, known as Fair Oaks or Seven Pines, 5,000 Union soldiers and 6,100 Confederate soldiers lost their lives. There was no clear victory for either side, but General Johnston was badly wounded. This led the way for General Robert E. Lee to take command of the Confederate forces.

THE SEVEN DAYS BATTLES

After the Battle of Fair Oaks, General Robert E. Lee sent 1,200 Confederate soldiers on horseback into northern Virginia to spy on General McClellan. For three days, Confederate cavalry officer J.E.B. Stuart led his men on a 150 mile ride. Along the way, they burned Union camps, took 170 prisoners, and stole 300 horses and mules. With the information that Stuart's men gathered, General Lee planned his next move.

On June 26, 1862, a week of battles began. Southern troops attacked Union forces, causing the Union troops to retreat. As they fled the area, the Union soldiers burned the bridge behind them. General McClellan moved his men back across the Virginia Peninsula toward an area known as Harrison's Landing.

During the next two days, General Lee's men chased McClellan's Union troops through the swampy region. Neither side claimed victory, but McClellan found a safe spot high on top of Malvern Hill. He planned to meet his enemy head on.

THE BATTLE OF MALVERN HILL

General McClellan placed his Union troops under the command of Major General Fitz Porter. Defending Malvern Hill would be easy for the Union; a swamp at the base of the hill kept the Confederate forces from spreading out. On the evening of July 1, 1862, Confederate General Robert E. Lee launched his **assault** up the hill. General Porter's Union troops fired cannonballs and bullets at the approaching Confederate troops. Confederate soldiers who made it up the hill were taken as prisoners.

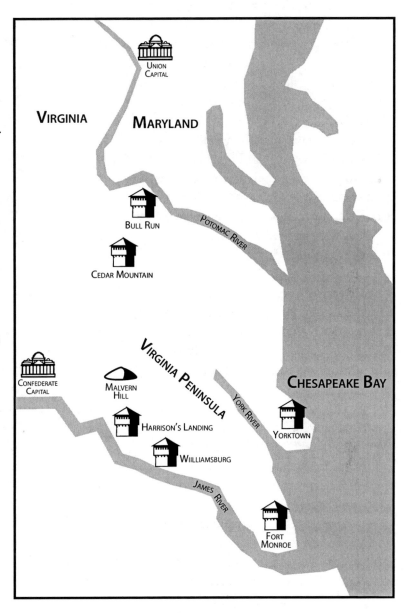

By the end of the day, 5,000 Union and Confederate soldiers had been wounded or killed. General Lee withdrew his troops from the battlefield and returned to the safety of Richmond.

Instead of capturing Lee's Confederate soldiers, General McClellan ordered his Union troops to abandon Malvern Hill and return to Harrison's Landing.

Many historians believe that allowing General Lee and his army to return to Richmond was a costly mistake.

In August 1862, General McClellan returned to Washington. His failure to capture Richmond forced President Lincoln to replace McClellan. General John Pope was chosen to command the Army of the Potomac.

Pope was a West Point graduate who had proven his bravery in the Mexican War. He promised President Lincoln that if given the chance, he would defeat General Robert E. Lee.

THE BATTLE OF CEDAR MOUNTAIN

Confederate General Robert E. Lee listened closely to reports about the Union's new leader, General John Pope. General Lee sent Thomas "Stonewall" Jackson and a force of 14,000 men to spy on General Pope. They found Pope commanding 50,000 Union soldiers in eastern Virginia. A short battle broke out at Cedar Mountain. Jackson was able to **rally** his men to a Confederate victory.

THE SECOND BATTLE OF BULL RUN

Two days later, General Pope found "Stonewall" Jackson and his men near the **former** Bull Run battle site. General Pope was sure that his Union troops outnumbered Jackson's Confederate armies. Pope believed that the battle would be a quick victory. General Pope didn't know it at the time, but General Lee's troops had joined Jackson's Confederate forces.

General Pope's Union soldiers fought hard. At one point during the battle, the Confederate troops ran out of ammunition and threw rocks at their enemies.

During the second day of battle, Pope attacked Jackson's men again. To the Union's surprise, 30,000 fresh Confederate soldiers were on the battlefield! As the Union retreated from the battle, the Confederate soldiers showered them with bullets.

Once again, the Confederacy claimed victory at Bull Run. It was a costly battle for both sides. The Union lost 16,000 men, while 10,000 Confederate soldiers lost their lives.

The summer of 1862 had been very successful for General Robert E. Lee and his Confederate troops. Western Virginia was in control of the Confederacy. The capital at Richmond was safe.

General Pope was **demoted** and sent to handle Native American attacks in Minnesota. He never fought in the Civil War again. Running low on skilled commanders, President Lincoln once again assigned General George McClellan to command the Army of the Potomac.

THOMAS "STONEWALL" JACKSON

THE EASTERN THEATER

Directions: Read each question carefully. Darken the circle for the correct answer.

1 During the Peninsula Campaign, General George McClellan planned to –

A capture the Confederacy's capital in Richmond

B take control of the Mississippi River

C capture New Orleans

D move his army into Kentucky, Louisiana, Missouri, and Tennessee

2 After reading about the Battle of Yorktown, you get the idea that –

F General McClellan could be easily fooled into believing something that was not true

G General Magruder was not a very smart man

H General Magruder panicked and surrendered Yorktown without a fight

J McClellan and his men took control of Yorktown

3 During the Battle of Fair Oaks, why didn't President Lincoln send 40,000 troops to help General McClellan?

A President Lincoln didn't know General McClellan needed more men.

B President Lincoln did send 40,000 men to help General McClellan; they got lost and never arrived.

C President Lincoln felt the troops were needed to guard the Union's capital.

D General McClellan told President Lincoln that he didn't need any extra troops.

4 What mistake did General McClellan make during the Battle of Malvern Hill?

F He told his men not to fire their cannons.

G His men didn't take any Confederate prisoners.

H He allowed General Lee and his army to return to the safety of Richmond.

J He captured the Confederate capital.

5 What can you learn by studying the Battle of Malvern Hill map?

A Malvern Hill is east of the Chesapeake Bay.

B The Union capital is south of the Potomac River.

C Williamsburg is northwest of Fort Monroe.

D Harrison's Landing is east of the York River.

6 What important piece of information would have helped General Pope during the Second Battle of Bull Run?

F Knowing exactly how many Confederate soldiers he was fighting against.

G Where to find the Confederate capital.

H The exact location of Thomas "Stonewall" Jackson and his men.

J President Lincoln's phone number.

Answers   READING

1 Ⓐ Ⓑ Ⓒ Ⓓ   4 Ⓕ Ⓖ Ⓗ Ⓙ
2 Ⓕ Ⓖ Ⓗ Ⓙ   5 Ⓐ Ⓑ Ⓒ Ⓓ
3 Ⓐ Ⓑ Ⓒ Ⓓ   6 Ⓕ Ⓖ Ⓗ Ⓙ

Name _____

The Eastern Theater

While the Western Theater was going very well for the Union, the Eastern Theater was not as successful. Read the questions below about the Eastern Theater. Write your answers on the lines provided. Attach a separate piece of paper if you need more room. Be ready to discuss some of your answers.

- **By the end of 1862, Union troops in the West had captured important states and forts along the Mississippi River. In the East, the Union was having difficulty taking control of the Confederate capital.**

  Why do you think the Western Theater was successful, while the Union Army was failing in the East?

  _____

  _____

  _____

  If you had been President Lincoln, what would you have done differently to help the Union Army be more successful in the Eastern Theater?

  _____

  _____

  _____

- **Many historians believe that allowing General Lee and his Confederate troops to return to the safety of Richmond was a big mistake.**

  Why do you think General McClellan let General Lee and his army return to Richmond? Do you agree or do you think General McClellan should have done something else?

  _____

  _____

  _____

  _____

THE BATTLE OF YORKTOWN

Since the beginning of the Civil War, the

Union's goal was to _____

_____

During the Battle of Yorktown, the Union

troops were led by _____

The Confederate troops were led by _____

The Confederates tricked the Union into thinking there were more soldiers

guarding Yorktown by _____

_____

_____

Instead of attacking, the Union leader telegraphed President Lincoln and told

him _____

_____

Victory for the Battle of Yorktown went to_____

One interesting fact about the Battle of Yorktown is _____

_____

_____

_____

_____

_____

_____

THE BATTLE OF FAIR OAKS

One month after the Battle of Yorktown, General George B. McClellan was ready to try again to

_____

_____

Five miles from Richmond, General McClellan panicked because _____

_____

_____

During the Battle of Fair Oaks, the Union troops were led by General McClellan. The Confederate troops were led by _____

_____

Victory for the Battle of Fair Oaks went to

_____

GEORGE B. MCCLELLAN

One interesting fact about the Battle of Fair Oaks is_____

_____

_____

_____

_____

_____

_____

THE BATTLE OF MALVERN HILL

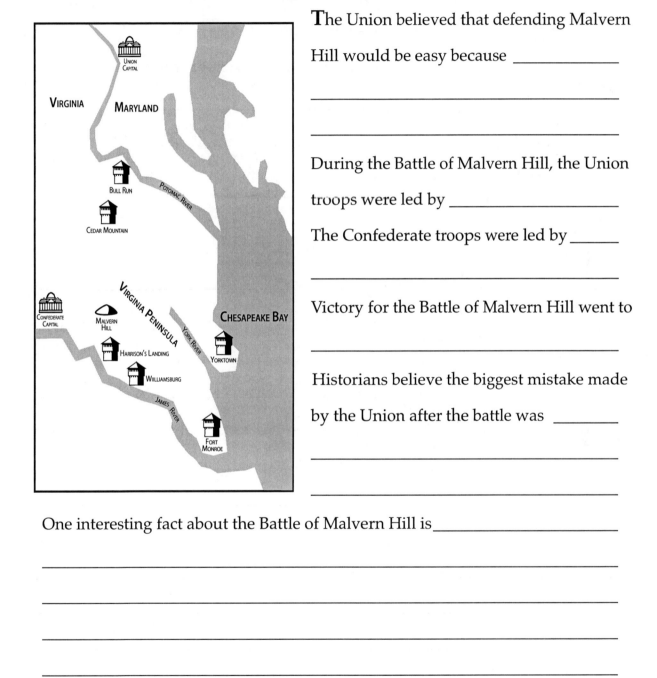

The Union believed that defending Malvern Hill would be easy because _____

_____

_____

During the Battle of Malvern Hill, the Union troops were led by _____

The Confederate troops were led by _____

_____

Victory for the Battle of Malvern Hill went to

_____

Historians believe the biggest mistake made by the Union after the battle was _____

_____

_____

One interesting fact about the Battle of Malvern Hill is_____

_____

_____

_____

_____

_____

_____

After the Battle of Cedar Mountain, the

Confederate troops were found near

_____

_____

Union General John Pope thought a battle would

be quick because _____

_____

_____

General Pope didn't know it at the time, but

_____

_____

During the second day of battle, the Union was

surprised by _____

ROBERT E. LEE

_____

Victory for the Second Battle of Bull Run went to _____

One interesting fact about the Second Battle of Bull Run is _____

_____

_____

_____

_____

_____

INVASION OF THE NORTH

In the beginning of the Civil War, President Lincoln was more concerned about putting the United States back together than ending slavery. Although President Lincoln hated slavery, he was still afraid that the border states of Missouri, Kentucky, Maryland, and Delaware would secede from the Union if they were forced to give up their slaves. He also feared that the Northern troops would refuse to fight if the war became an issue of slavery instead of reuniting the Union. In addition, President Lincoln was not sure blacks and whites would ever be able to live side by side in the United States.

In March 1862, Congress abolished slavery in Washington, D.C. Union Army leaders were ordered not to return captured slaves to their Southern plantations. Two months later, Congress also **banned** slavery in the western territories.

BLACK SOLDIERS

The first shots of the Civil War set off a rush of free black men who wanted to volunteer for the Union Army. They had been turned away. Although many black soldiers had fought in the American Revolution and the War of 1812, President Lincoln feared that the white Union soldiers would not want to fight alongside black troops.

By the middle of 1862, the Union was in need of fresh soldiers. Thousands of slaves were being set free as the Union took control of Confederate states. President Lincoln changed his mind and decided to allow blacks to fight. In July 1862, black Americans were accepted into the Union Army and Navy.

Black volunteers were paid $200 if they served in the Union Army or Navy for 20 months. They were also promised freedom for themselves and for their families. Black soldiers were paid less than white soldiers. Unlike white soldiers, blacks were forced to pay for their uniforms. They were separated from white soldiers and were usually commanded in their black units by white officers.

Black troops who were captured by the Confederate Army were treated much more **harshly** than white prisoners.

BLACK CIVIL WAR SOLDIER

Black captives were beaten, shot to death, or forced back into a life of slavery. The fear of mistreatment and death did not keep blacks from volunteering. Almost 200,000 black men volunteered to fight in the Union Army and Navy.

GENERAL LEE INVADES MARYLAND

In September 1862, General Robert E. Lee made the bold move of marching his Confederate troops North into Maryland. General Lee hoped that a successful invasion on Union soil would convince England or France to support the Confederacy and send much needed supplies and troops.

On September 4, 1862, with 50,000 men and 300 cannons, General Lee crossed the Potomac River. He divided his army into parts, spreading his troops across Pennsylvania, Virginia, and Maryland. General Lee marched his group of 18,000 soldiers into the small town of Frederick, Maryland. General McClellan heard about Lee's divided army and immediately sent 100,000 Union troops to greet him.

Once again, General McClellan moved too slowly. By the time McClellan arrived, General Lee was able to gather 30,000 men, with more on the way. General Lee grouped his men at Sharpsburg, a town in western Maryland.

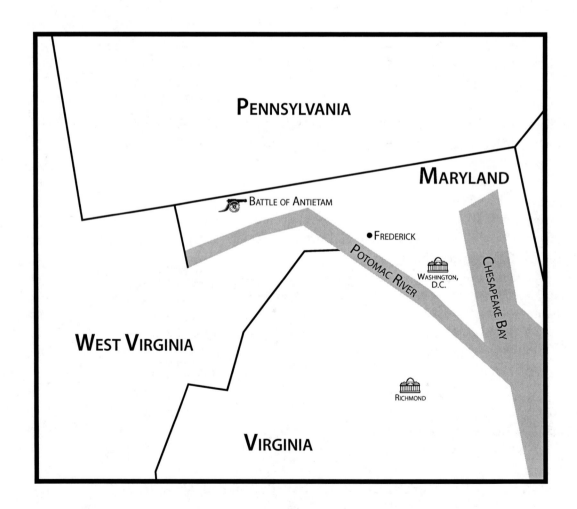

THE BATTLE OF ANTIETAM (AN•TEE•TUM)

On September 16, 1862, General Lee's Confederate troops moved into position north and east of Sharpsburg. They were hiding in the woods, a cornfield, a sunken roadway, and on a bridge that overlooked Antietam Creek.

At dawn the next morning, General McClellan's troops charged into the cornfield. Within minutes, bodies from both sides littered the battlefield. By the middle of the day, the Union Army had forced the Confederates to fall back toward the town. The sunken roadway had become a bloody lane. Late in the afternoon, the Union soldiers made their way across the bridge. General Lee's reinforcements arrived just in time. The Union was forced to retreat.

General Lee stayed in position the next day to see if McClellan and his Union troops would attack again. Although McClellan's troops still outnumbered General Lee's armies, the Union general chose not to attack. General Lee took his army back to Virginia.

The Union claimed victory for the Battle of Antietam, ending General Lee's first invasion of the North. The Battle of Antietam was the bloodiest single day of the entire Civil War. More than 23,000 soldiers from the two armies were dead or wounded. General Lee lost almost one quarter of his army in just one day. He also lost the support of England and France. Neither country was willing to join the Confederacy after the loss at Antietam.

THE EMANCIPATION PROCLAMATION

After the Union victory at Antietam, President Lincoln made a bold move. He announced that if the **rebellion** didn't end, all slaves in the Confederacy would be freed. On January 1, 1863, President Lincoln issued the final **Emancipation Proclamation**. After this date, every time the Union troops **conquered** a Confederate territory, the black slaves were freed. The Emancipation Proclamation gave instant freedom to about three million people. Many of the free slaves immediately joined the Union and fought to end slavery permanently.

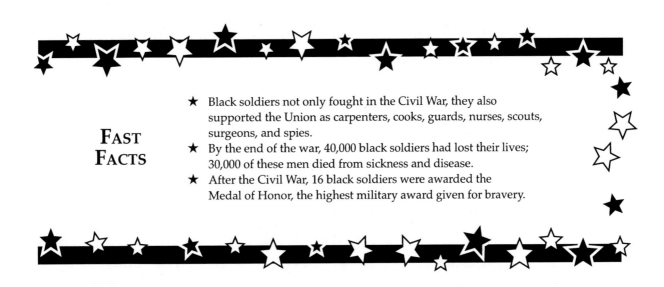

FAST FACTS

★ Black soldiers not only fought in the Civil War, they also supported the Union as carpenters, cooks, guards, nurses, scouts, surgeons, and spies.

★ By the end of the war, 40,000 black soldiers had lost their lives; 30,000 of these men died from sickness and disease.

★ After the Civil War, 16 black soldiers were awarded the Medal of Honor, the highest military award given for bravery.

★ ★ INVASION OF THE NORTH ★ ★

Directions: Read each question carefully. Darken the circle for the correct answer.

---

1   In the beginning of the Civil War, President Lincoln was most concerned with –

A   abolishing slavery

B   freeing slaves in all of the Confederate states

C   bringing the United States back together

D   getting elected as president of the United States for a second time

2   After reading about black soldiers, you learn that –

F   they were treated the same as white soldiers

G   they were not paid for fighting in the Civil War

H   black soldiers did not want to fight in the Civil War

J   fear of mistreatment or death did not keep black men from volunteering to fight for the Union Army and Navy

3   Why did Robert E. Lee make the bold move of invading the North?

A   He was tired of being attacked on Confederate soil in the South.

B   He knew his troops outnumbered General McClellan's troops.

C   He hoped that winning battles in the North would convince England or France to help the Confederacy.

D   He was hiding from General McClellan.

4   According to the map of the North, Richmond is –

F   in Maryland

G   east of the Potomac River

H   west of the Chesapeake Bay

J   in Pennsylvania

5   All of the following statements about the Battle of Antietam are false except –

A   the Confederacy claimed victory for the Battle of Antietam

B   General Robert E. Lee was killed during the Battle of Antietam

C   England and France supported the Confederacy after the Battle of Antietam

D   the Battle of Antietam was the bloodiest single day of the entire Civil War

6   The Emancipation Proclamation –

F   was announced by General Grant

G   freed all of the slaves in the Confederate territories captured by the Union

H   was announced after the Confederate victory at Antietam

J   paid slave owners for giving their slaves freedom

READING

Answers

1   Ⓐ Ⓑ Ⓒ Ⓓ   4   Ⓕ Ⓖ Ⓗ Ⓙ

2   Ⓕ Ⓖ Ⓗ Ⓙ   5   Ⓐ Ⓑ Ⓒ Ⓓ

3   Ⓐ Ⓑ Ⓒ Ⓓ   6   Ⓕ Ⓖ Ⓗ Ⓙ

THE BATTLE OF ANTIETAM

On September 16, 1862, Confederate troops moved into position north and east of

_____

in the state of _____

They were hiding in _____

_____

At the end of the first day of the Battle of Antietam, the Union was forced to _____

The Union troops were led by

_____

The Confederate troops were led by _____

_____

Victory for the Battle of Antietam went to

BLACK CIVIL WAR SOLDIER

_____

One interesting fact about the Battle of Antietam is _____

_____

_____

_____

_____

_____

_____

Geography is the study of the Earth. It includes the Earth's land, water, weather, animal life, and plant life. **Geographers** are people who study geography. You can think of yourself as a geographer because you will be learning about places on the Earth.

Location is important to the study of geography. It is almost impossible to figure out your location or find your way around if you do not know the four main, or **cardinal directions.** North, south, east, and west are the **cardinal directions**. On a map these directions are labeled N, S, E, and W.

COMPASS ROSE

Between the four main directions are the **intermediate directions.** Northeast, or NE, is the direction between north and east. Southeast, or SE, is the direction between south and east. Southwest, or SW, is the direction between south and west. Northwest, or NW, is the direction between north and west.

A **reference point** is also important for finding your location. A **reference point** is simply a starting point. It's difficult, for example, to travel southeast if you don't have a starting point.

Example: The Battle of Big Bethel was fought on June 10, 1861. Historians believe this was the first land battle of the Eastern Theater. Although the Union outnumbered the Confederates two to one, the Union was disorganized and had to flee the area. The Battle of Big Bethel was fought <u>southeast</u> of <u>Richmond</u>.

This example gives you some very important information. It tells you that your **reference point**, or starting point, will be the city of Richmond. Locate Richmond on your Eastern Theater map. Put your finger on Richmond and slide it <u>southeast</u>. You should see a picture of the Battle of Big Bethel already placed there for you.

Sometimes directions contain more than one **reference point**. Look at the example below:

Example: The Battle of Corrick's **Ford** was fought on July 13, 1861. The Union victory ended a series of battles between Union General George B. McClellan and Confederate Brigadier General Robert S. Garnett. The Battle of Corrick's Ford was fought <u>northeast</u> of <u>Charleston</u> and <u>southwest</u> of the city of <u>Keyser</u>.

This example contains two **reference points** and two sets of directions. They have been underlined for you. Look at your Eastern Theater map. Put your finger on the city of <u>Charleston</u> and slide it <u>northeast</u>. Since there are many battle sites located northeast, a second **reference point** has been added to help you find your location.

The second **reference point** is <u>Keyser</u>. Place your finger on the city of <u>Keyser</u> and slide it <u>southwest</u>. By using both of these **reference points**, you should be able to easily locate the Battle of Corrick's Ford.

Directions: In this activity you will use reference points, cardinal directions, and intermediate directions to plot important Eastern Theater battles during the first two years of the Civil War.

1.   Label the cardinal and intermediate directions on the compass rose drawn for you on the blank Eastern Theater map.

2.   Use your scissors to carefully cut out the symbols on the bottom of the last page.

3.   Use the written directions and your compass rose to correctly locate the battles on your Eastern Theater map.

4.   To get you started, the reference points and directions have been underlined for you in the first five descriptions. You may want to underline the reference points and directions in the rest of the activity.

5.   Glue the symbols in their proper places on your map. (Glue the symbols right over the dots.)

6.   If a battle was a Confederate victory, color the box around the symbol red. If the battle was a Union victory, color the box around the symbol blue. (You will need to color in the boxes for the two examples already placed for you on the map.)

7.   When you have finished, ask your teacher to pull down the classroom map of the United States. Neatly label each state on the map with its correct name. Spelling counts!

8.   Use your coloring pencils to add more color to your Eastern Theater map.

1. The Battle of Hoke's Run was fought on July 2, 1861. During the battle, the Union forces pushed back Thomas "Stonewall" Jackson's troops, allowing Major General Robert Patterson and his Union soldiers to march toward Bunker Hill. The Battle of Hoke's Run was fought <u>east</u> of the city of <u>Keyser</u>.

2. The Battle of Bull Run was fought on July 21, 1861. The Confederate victory was the first major land battle of the Civil War. The Battle of Bull Run was fought <u>west</u> of <u>Arlington</u> and <u>southeast</u> of the <u>Battle of Hoke's Run</u>.

3. The Battle of Carnifex Ferry was fought on September 10, 1861. The battle resulted in a Union victory, forcing the Confederates to completely withdraw from the area. The Battle of Carnifex Ferry was fought <u>southeast</u> of <u>Charleston</u> and <u>north</u> of the city of <u>Lewisburg</u>.

4. The Battle of Cheat Mountain took place between September 12 and September 15, 1861. Confederate General Robert E. Lee divided his men into three groups and attacked the Union troops on Cheat Mountain. Rain, fog, and **mountainous** terrain forced the Confederates to call off the attack, leaving the victory for the battle to the Union. The Battle of Cheat Mountain was fought <u>south</u> of the <u>Battle of Corrick's Ford</u> and <u>east</u> of <u>Charleston</u>.

5. The Battle of Ball's Bluff was fought on October 21, 1861. Though it was a minor battle compared to others that were fought during the Civil War, the Battle of Ball's Bluff was the second largest battle of the Eastern Theater in 1861. The Union was defeated and unable to take control of the Potomac River as it had hoped. The Battle of Ball's Bluff was fought <u>southeast</u> of the <u>Battle of Hoke's Run</u> and <u>northwest</u> of <u>Arlington</u>.

6. The Battle of McDowell was fought from May 8 to May 9, 1862. During the four hour battle that claimed more than 700 lives, the Union retreated. The Confederate victory allowed Thomas "Stonewall" Jackson's forces to attack other Union troops in the area. The Battle of McDowell was fought southeast of the Battle of Carnifex Ferry and southwest of the city of Harrisonburg.

7. The Battle of Drewry's Bluff was fought on May 15, 1862. Five Union Navy gunboats steamed up the James River to see how well the Confederates were protecting their capital in Richmond. Cannons from Drewry's Bluff fired repeatedly at the Navy's ships, severely damaging one of them. The Union Navy was forced to turn back, giving the Confederates the victory for the battle. The Battle of Drewry's Bluff was fought southwest of Richmond.

8. The Battle of Cross Keys was fought on June 8, 1862. The Confederate victory by Thomas "Stonewall" Jackson and his men forced the Union armies to retreat. This allowed Stonewall Jackson to join General Robert E. Lee during the important Seven Days' Battles. The Battle of Cross Keys was fought west of the Battle of Bull Run.

9. The Seven Days' Battles were six major battles fought from June 25 to July 1, 1862. The week long fighting ended with a Confederate victory. Union forces, led by General George McClellan were forced to retreat to the safety of Malvern Hill. The Seven Days' Battles were fought northeast of Richmond.

10. The Battle of Malvern Hill took place on July 1, 1862. During the battle that wounded and killed more than 5,000 Union and Confederate soldiers, General Robert E. Lee and his Confederate troops were forced to withdraw and return to the safety of their capital in Richmond. The Battle of Malvern Hill was fought east of Richmond.

11. The Battle of Cedar Mountain was fought on August 9, 1862. In the beginning of the battle, it looked as though the Union might win. Not willing to be defeated, Confederate commander Thomas "Stonewall" Jackson rallied his troops to victory. The Battle of Cedar Mountain was fought southwest of the Seven Days' Battles and northeast of Harrisonburg.

12. The Battle of South Mountain was fought on September 14, 1862. Before the battle, Union General George McClellan had heard that Confederate General Robert E. Lee had divided his army into three parts. McClellan planned to attack Lee's forces while they were weak. It worked. General Lee commanded his outnumbered forces to withdraw, giving the Union a victory. The Battle of South Mountain was fought northwest of Washington, D.C. and northeast of the Battle of Hoke's Run.

13. The Battle of Antietam was fought on September 17, 1862. It was the first major battle in the Civil War to take place on Northern soil. With 23,000 soldiers dead or wounded, the Battle of Antietam was also the bloodiest single day of the Civil War. The Union claimed victory for the battle, ending General Robert E. Lee's first invasion of the North. The Battle of Antietam was fought northwest of the Battle of South Mountain.

Name _____

THE EASTERN THEATER 1861-1862

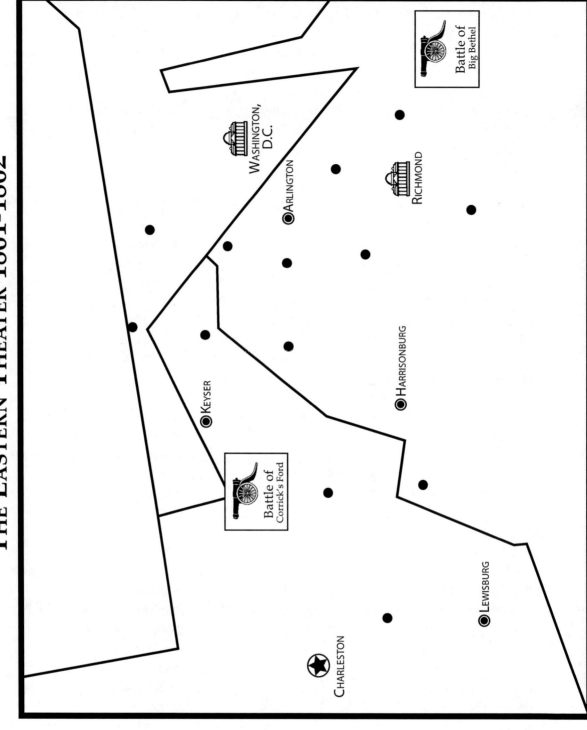

Battle of Big Bethel

WASHINGTON, D.C.

◉ARLINGTON

RICHMOND

HARRISONBURG ◉

KEYSER ◉

Battle of Corrick's Ford

LEWISBURG ◉

CHARLESTON ★

COMPASS ROSE

The Civil War © 2009
splashpublications.com

74

BATTLES OF 1863

The Battle of Antietam (an•TEE•tum) once again showed President Lincoln that General George McClellan was probably not the best choice to lead the Union to victory. Although the Union claimed victory at Antietam, McClellan had not crushed General Lee's army. Once again, McClellan had let General Lee escape to the safety of Richmond.

President Lincoln first replaced General McClellan with General Ambrose Burnside. After losing a battle and 13,000 men in Fredericksburg, Virginia, General Burnside was quickly replaced with Major General Joseph Hooker. Hooker's **aggressive** style of fighting earned him the nickname "Fighting Joe."

THE BATTLE OF CHANCELLORSVILLE

By the spring of 1863, General Hooker's Union Army of 130,000 was rested and confident. He led 70,000 of his men to Chancellorsville, a Virginia town northwest of Richmond. The other 60,000 soldiers stayed near Fredericksburg.

General Lee also left a small group of soldiers in Fredericksburg and moved the rest of his Confederate soldiers towards Chancellorsville. Near Chancellorsville, Lee split his army into two parts. He sent Thomas "Stonewall" Jackson and a large part of his Confederate troops to meet up with the Union Army.

On May 2, 1863, Jackson attacked. The Union troops panicked and scattered in different directions. General Hooker was able to bring his men back together before fighting ended for the day.

THE DEATH OF "STONEWALL" JACKSON

That night, Stonewall Jackson rode through the wilderness on horseback. As he returned to camp, he was shot by one of his own men who thought he was a member of the Union Army. Thomas "Stonewall" Jackson died eight days later.

General Lee put J.E.B. Stuart in command of Jackson's part of the Confederate Army. On May 3, 1863, Lee and Stuart led another attack on General Hooker and his Union troops. Hooker was wounded during the battle and ordered his men to pull back. "Fighting Joe" had lost his courage. The Confederate victory at Chancellorsville claimed the lives of 17,000 Union and 12,500 Confederate soldiers.

THE BATTLE OF GETTYSBURG

The Battle of Chancellorsville gave General Robert E. Lee the confidence to once again invade the North. He believed more than ever that the Confederate Army, though outnumbered in every battle, could not be beaten.

President Lincoln fired General Hooker and replaced him with General George Gordon Meade. In just a few days, Lincoln's new commander would have to lead the Union Army in one of the Civil War's toughest battles.

In July 1863, the Confederate and Union armies met at the same place in Gettysburg, Pennsylvania. The battle that broke out was unplanned and neither general had time to position his troops.

THE FIRST DAY AT GETTYSBURG

On July 1, 1863, Confederate soldiers marched toward Gettysburg in hopes of finding a supply of shoes stored there. Instead of finding shoes, the Confederates found the Union cavalry. A fierce battle broke out with soldiers no more than 20 feet apart firing at one another. As new soldiers arrived, they were thrown into the battle.

By nightfall, the Union troops were forced to retreat to Cemetery Ridge, an area of hills that stretched from the town of Gettysburg to the south. It was decided that the ridge and its two hills would make good protection for the Union troops. General Lee positioned his Confederate troops north and west of General Meade's Union forces.

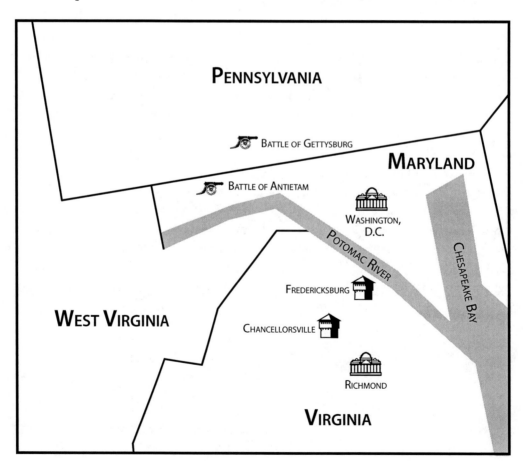

THE SECOND DAY AT GETTYSBURG

During the second day of fighting, General Lee ordered his men to attack from the north and south. The plan failed. General Meade sent reinforcements into the area and stopped the Confederates from taking control. By the end of the second day, neither side was able to claim victory for Gettysburg.

THE THIRD DAY AT GETTYSBURG

On the third day of fighting, 15,000 of General Lee's Confederate troops attacked the Union in the center of Cemetery Ridge. Lee's officers disagreed with his plan of attack, but General Lee ordered it anyway. By early afternoon on July 3, nearly 170 Confederate cannons were pounding away at the Union line to weaken its defenses.

The Union troops returned fire, blasting away at the Confederate forces. By the end of the day, the victory belonged to the Union. General Lee withdrew his men from Gettysburg. Once again, the Union outnumbered the Confederacy. General Meade could have crushed General Lee. General Meade refused to continue the attack against the weakened Confederate troops.

More than 50,000 men were wounded, missing, or lost their lives during the three day Battle of Gettysburg. It would go down in history as the largest battle ever fought in North America. It would also be the last time that the Confederates would invade the North. From that point forward, the Confederacy would have to fight the Civil War on its own soil in the South.

THE GETTYSBURG ADDRESS

After the Battle of Gettysburg, several Northern governors created a cemetery to honor those who had died during the battle. On November 19, 1863, a **dedication** ceremony was held. During the ceremony, President Lincoln gave his famous Gettysburg Address.

In his speech, President Lincoln explained the meaning of the Battle of Gettysburg and the reason for the Civil War. He reminded everyone that our nation had been **founded** on the idea that "all men are created equal." President Lincoln said that the Civil War was being fought to protect our nation and the freedom of all people.

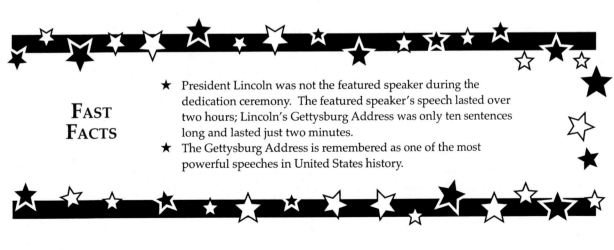

FAST FACTS

★ President Lincoln was not the featured speaker during the dedication ceremony. The featured speaker's speech lasted over two hours; Lincoln's Gettysburg Address was only ten sentences long and lasted just two minutes.
★ The Gettysburg Address is remembered as one of the most powerful speeches in United States history.

THE BATTLE OF VICKSBURG

While the Battle of Gettysburg was raging in Pennsylvania, an important battle was taking place in the Mississippi town of Vicksburg. Vicksburg was important because it was located right on the Mississippi River. Complete control of the Mississippi River was necessary to win the war.

On May 16, 1863, Union General Ulysses S. Grant marched 70,000 soldiers towards Vicksburg. The Union troops surrounded the town. For 66 days, the Union bombed the small town. The citizens of Vicksburg dug caves and tunnels into the hillsides to serve as bomb shelters. Without a way to get food and supplies, the people of Vicksburg began to starve to death. Soldiers and **civilians** were forced to eat their mules, pets, and even rats.

On July 4, 1863, the day after the victory at Gettysburg, the town of Vicksburg finally surrendered. For the first time during the Civil War, the Union was in complete control of the Mississippi River.

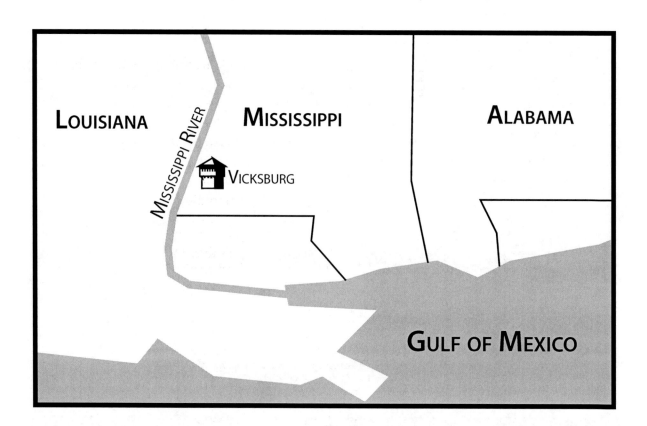

Name _____

★ ★ ★ BATTLES OF 1863 ★ ★ ★

Directions: Read each question carefully. Darken the circle for the correct answer.

1 **After winning the Battle of Antietam, why did President Lincoln replace General McClellan with another commander?**

A McClellan was tired of fighting for the Union.

B Commanders had to be replaced after every battle.

C Once again, McClellan let General Lee escape to the safety of Richmond.

D McClellan demanded too much money for commanding the Union Army.

2 **How did Thomas "Stonewall" Jackson die?**

F He was shot by General Joseph Hooker.

G He was shot by one of his own men.

H He fell off his horse and broke his neck.

J He died during the Battle of Chancellorsville.

3 **According to the map on the second page, the Battle of Gettysburg was fought –**

A south of Washington, D.C.

B west of the Battle of Antietam

C in West Virginia

D northeast of the Battle of Antietam

4 **By studying the map, you learn that Washington, D.C. is –**

F in Maryland

G west of the Potomac River

H east of the Chesapeake Bay

J in Pennsylvania

5 **How were General McClellan and General Meade alike?**

A Neither man had won a victory for the Union Army.

B Both men were killed during battle.

C Neither commander lost a single man during battle.

D Neither took advantage of crushing his enemy when he had the chance.

6 **During the Gettysburg Address, President Lincoln –**

F reminded everyone that in our nation, all men are created equal

G gave the longest speech in history

H refused to continue fighting the Civil War

J admitted that he was not sure why we were fighting the Civil War

7 **How did the Union win the Battle of Vicksburg?**

A General Grant paid the people of Vicksburg to surrender.

B The Union Army surrounded the town and waited for the people to surrender.

C Union soldiers attacked the town by flying over in airplanes.

D Everyone in Vicksburg ran away as soon as they found out the Union Army was on its way.

READING

Answers

1 Ⓐ Ⓑ Ⓒ Ⓓ	5 Ⓐ Ⓑ Ⓒ Ⓓ
2 Ⓕ Ⓖ Ⓗ Ⓙ	6 Ⓕ Ⓖ Ⓗ Ⓙ
3 Ⓐ Ⓑ Ⓒ Ⓓ	7 Ⓐ Ⓑ Ⓒ Ⓓ
4 Ⓕ Ⓖ Ⓗ Ⓙ	

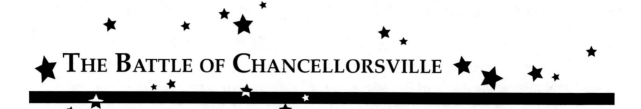

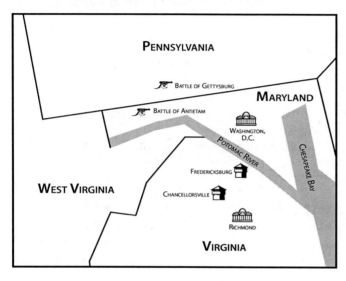

After replacing General George McClellan with General Ambrose Burnside, President Lincoln finally settled on

_____

to lead the Union Army. This leader's aggressive style of fighting earned him the

nickname_____

During the Battle of Chancellorsville, the Confederate troops were led by

_____

He split his army into two pieces and sent a large part of his troops with

_____ to meet up with the Union Army.

Victory for the Battle of Chancellorsville went to _____

One interesting fact about the Battle of Chancellorsville is _____

_____

_____

_____

_____

_____

_____

★ THE BATTLE OF GETTYSBURG ★

The Battle of Chancellorsville gave General Robert E.

Lee the confidence to _____

In July 1863, the Confederate and Union armies met in

_____

The Union troops were led by _____

_____

The Confederate troops were led by _____

_____

By the end of the third day of fighting, victory for the

Battle of Gettysburg belonged to _____

Instead of crushing the Confederate Army, the Union

commander _____

_____

ABRAHAM LINCOLN

After the Battle of Gettysburg, President Lincoln gave

his famous speech entitled _____

One interesting fact about the Battle of Gettysburg is_____

_____

_____

_____

_____

_____

THE BATTLE OF VICKSBURG

While the Battle of Gettysburg was raging in Pennsylvania, an important battle was taking place in Vicksburg, Mississippi. Vicksburg was important because

_____

_____

_____

_____

Complete control of the Mississippi River was necessary to _____

_____

To gain control of Vicksburg, the Union Army _____

_____

Without a way to get food and supplies, the people of Vicksburg _____

_____

One interesting fact about the Battle of Vicksburg is _____

_____

_____

_____

_____

_____

BATTLES OF 1864

By the end of 1863, both the Union and the Confederacy were suffering. The Union victory at Gettysburg had ended the Confederate invasion of the North forever. The Battle of Vicksburg gave the Union complete control of the Mississippi River. The Confederacy was short on soldiers, supplies, and ammunition. France and England were not interested in helping the Confederacy win a war against slavery.

Although the battles in 1863 had gone well for the Union, many Northerners were tired of the war. They questioned President Lincoln's leadership abilities. After Lincoln's Emancipation Proclamation, which freed all of the slaves in the Confederacy, some Northerners refused to support the war or President Lincoln. **Riots** broke out in New York City. A group called the Copperheads wanted to give the Southern states their independence so the war could end.

GENERAL GRANT TAKES COMMAND

As 1863 turned into 1864, President Lincoln realized that the Union needed a leader that was as strong as the Confederate's Robert E. Lee. On March 9, 1864, Ulysses S. Grant took command of the entire Union Army. General Grant told President Lincoln, "Whatever happens, there will be no turning back."

General Grant's strategy was simple. He planned to split the entire Union Army into parts and attack the Confederates in different places at the same time. During the first few months under General Grant's command, the Union Army lost more than 40,000 men. The Confederates only lost 25,000 men.

One Confederate soldier described General Grant as a leader "who either does not know when he is whipped, or who cares not if he loses his whole army." General Grant knew that losing 40,000 men was horrible. He also knew that the Confederacy would have a very difficult time replacing the soldiers it had lost in battle.

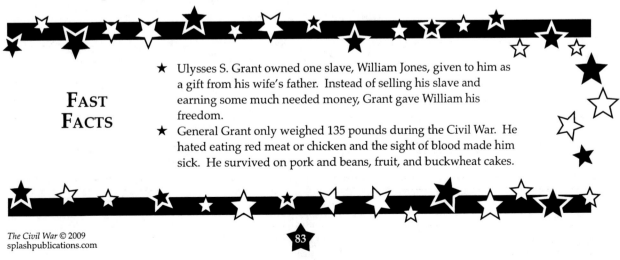

FAST FACTS

★ Ulysses S. Grant owned one slave, William Jones, given to him as a gift from his wife's father. Instead of selling his slave and earning some much needed money, Grant gave William his freedom.

★ General Grant only weighed 135 pounds during the Civil War. He hated eating red meat or chicken and the sight of blood made him sick. He survived on pork and beans, fruit, and buckwheat cakes.

THE BATTLES FOR ATLANTA

In May 1864, Union General William Tecumseh Sherman left Chattanooga, Tennessee. He marched 100,000 Union soldiers toward Atlanta, Georgia. Atlanta was the Confederacy's most important railroad and manufacturing center. Supplies and ammunition made in Atlanta were transported all over the South. Along the way to Atlanta, General Grant wanted Sherman to destroy Confederate crops and kill farm animals so the Confederacy would have no way to feed its troops.

General Sherman and his forces followed Confederate General Joseph Johnston and his 62,000 soldiers south through Tennessee and into Georgia. By early July, Johnston's Confederate troops had been chased into Atlanta. Many battles had been fought along the way, but General Johnston never attacked. This worried Confederate President Jefferson Davis, who wanted Johnston to be more aggressive. President Davis replaced General Johnston with John Bell Hood, a tough fighter from Robert E. Lee's army.

General Hood's troops were outnumbered in Atlanta. Still, he chose to attack General Sherman's Union troops three different times. In total, the Confederates lost about 20,000 men. General Sherman and his troops surrounded the city of Atlanta. They cut the city off from food, water, and supplies. By September 2, 1864, the city of Atlanta was completely under the Union's control.

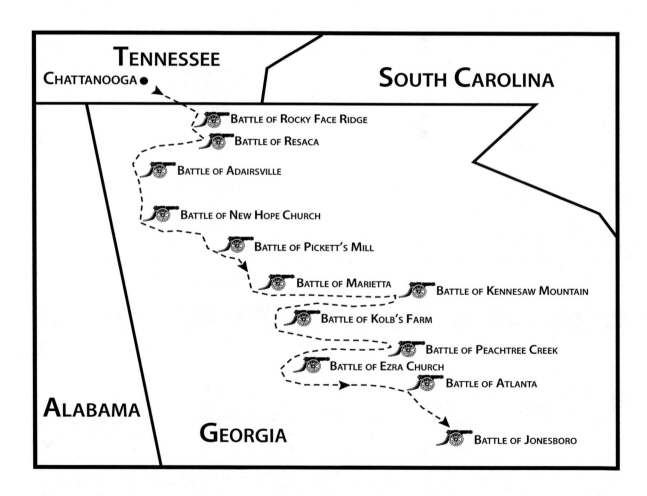

Sherman's March to the Sea

On November 15, 1864, General Sherman began his famous "March to the Sea." He took his 60,000 Union troops from Atlanta to the Georgia **seaport** of Savannah. For weeks, Sherman's men destroyed everything in their paths. They raided farms, plantations, and burned entire towns to the ground. Railroad lines, telegraph poles, and factories were destroyed. As they marched toward Savannah, Sherman's troops were joined by thousands of freed slaves.

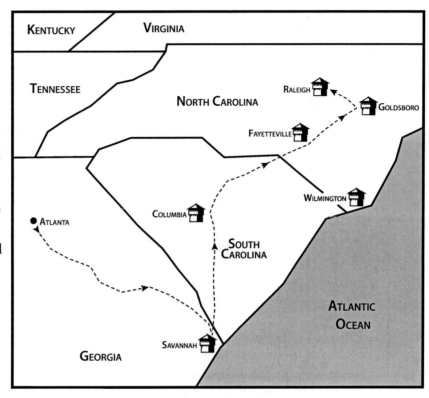

On December 21, 1864, Sherman and his men reached Savannah. They **plundered** the Confederate city, taking guns, ammunition, and 25,000 bales of cotton. Sherman and his Union soldiers then turned north and headed into South Carolina.

By February 17, 1865, General Sherman had taken control of Columbia, the state's capital. As they had done in Georgia, Sherman's men burned down every Confederate house, barn, and **mill** that they passed.

A week later, Union troops under the command of General Jacob Cox captured Wilmington, North Carolina. Wilmington was the only major North Carolina port not under Union control. For the next two months, Sherman's troops took control of the North Carolina towns of Fayetteville and Goldsboro. On April 13, 1865, they entered Raleigh, North Carolina.

The Siege on Richmond

While General Sherman made his way from Georgia to North Carolina, General Grant set his sights on finally capturing the Confederacy's capital in Richmond, Virginia. First, he planned to take control of Petersburg, Virginia. The railroads in Petersburg carried important supplies to General Lee's Confederate troops and the Confederate capital. If General Grant could capture Petersburg, he could cut off those supply lines.

On June 15, 1864, Grant's Union troops reached Petersburg. Instead of attacking, General Grant had his men dig miles and miles of **trenches** around the towns of Richmond and Petersburg, trapping the Confederate Army inside. Then they waited for the Confederates to surrender.

As the **siege** continued from month to month, General Grant brought in reinforcements and fresh supplies. General Lee's troops, on the other hand, were trapped inside of the towns. They couldn't get food or supplies. Things were not looking good for the Confederacy.

Name _____

★ ★ ★ BATTLES OF 1864 ★ ★ ★

Directions: Read each question carefully. Darken the circle for the correct answer.

1   All of the following phrases describe how some Northerners were feeling at the beginning of 1864, <u>except</u> –

   A   ...tired of the war...

   B   ...questioned President Lincoln's leadership abilities...

   C   ...refused to support the war...

   D   ...wanted the Confederacy to win the war...

2   When General Ulysses S. Grant took command of the Union Army –

   F   he didn't really have a plan of attack

   G   he wanted to keep the Union Army together and attack all at once

   H   he lost almost twice as many men as the Confederacy during his first few months as commander

   J   he told President Lincoln that he wasn't as strong as Robert E. Lee

3   It might surprise you to learn that General Grant –

   A   was married

   B   graduated from West Point Military Academy with honors

   C   fought in the Mexican War

   D   hated the sight of blood

4   Why did the Union Army want to take control of Atlanta?

   F   It was the Confederacy's most important railroad and manufacturing center.

   G   The Confederate capital was located in Atlanta.

   H   President Jefferson Davis was visiting Atlanta and they wanted to capture him.

   J   Atlanta had more slaves than any other Confederate city.

5   What can you learn by studying the map of General Sherman's march toward Atlanta?

   A   The Battle of Adairsville was fought before the Battle of Rocky Face Ridge.

   B   General Sherman and his men traveled north from Chattanooga to Atlanta.

   C   The Battle of Jonesboro was fought after the Battle of Peachtree Creek.

   D   Chattanooga is in South Carolina.

6   Study the map of General Sherman's famous "March to the Sea" to decide which event took place <u>before</u> Sherman's army captured Columbia, South Carolina.

   F   Sherman and his men reached the seaport of Savannah.

   G   Sherman's troops took control of Fayetteville.

   H   The town on Goldsboro was captured by Sherman and his men.

   J   Sherman and his men entered Raleigh, North Carolina.

7   The siege on Richmond lasted for months. <u>Siege</u> means about the same thing as –

   A   surrender

   B   ignore

   C   surround

   D   defend

READING

Answers

1 Ⓐ Ⓑ Ⓒ Ⓓ   5 Ⓐ Ⓑ Ⓒ Ⓓ
2 Ⓕ Ⓖ Ⓗ Ⓙ   6 Ⓕ Ⓖ Ⓗ Ⓙ
3 Ⓐ Ⓑ Ⓒ Ⓓ   7 Ⓐ Ⓑ Ⓒ Ⓓ
4 Ⓕ Ⓖ Ⓗ Ⓙ

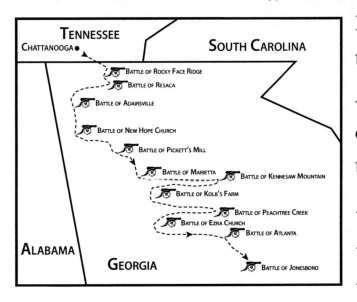

In May 1864, more than 100,000 Union troops headed toward Atlanta, Georgia. Gaining control of Atlanta was important to the Union because_____

_____

_____

_____

Along the way to Atlanta, the Union troops destroyed crops and killed farm animals so _____

_____

The Union troops were led by _____

The Confederate soldiers were led by _____

By September 2, 1864, the city of Atlanta was in complete control of _____

One interesting fact about the Battles for Atlanta is_____

_____

_____

_____

_____

_____

_____

★ SHERMAN'S MARCH TO THE SEA ★

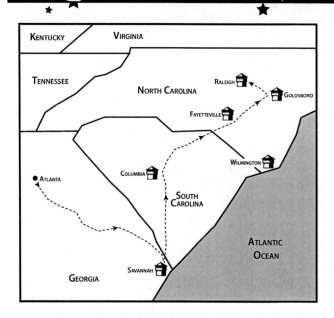

On November 15, 1864, General Sherman began his famous

_____

As they marched toward Savannah, Sherman's troops were joined by _____

_____

On December 21, 1864, Sherman and his men reached Savannah, Georgia. They plundered the city. Plundered means _____

Sherman and his men then turned north and headed into _____

By February 17, 1865, General Sherman had taken control of _____,

the state's capital. As they had done in Georgia, Sherman's men_____

_____

One interesting fact about Sherman's March to the Sea is_____

_____

_____

_____

_____

_____

_____

THE CIVIL WAR

Have you ever wondered what it would have been like to be alive during the Civil War? What part do you think you would have played in the war? Would you have been on the side of the Union or the Confederacy? Maybe you would have been a soldier, fighting on the front line. Or maybe you would have been a commander like General Robert E. Lee or General Ulysses S. Grant. Perhaps you would have been a doctor or nurse caring for the wounded. Imagine the stories you would have to tell your friends and family when you returned from the war.

Directions: Pretend you are part of the Civil War. Decide what part you play in the war. Write a letter to someone back home. Tell them about your adventures. Make sure that your letter includes:

HEADING, GREETING, BODY, CLOSING, SIGNATURE

- Before beginning your letter, organize your thoughts by answering the four questions on the next page.
- Write your rough draft on separate paper and have it edited.
- Write your final draft on the special paper provided by your teacher.
- When you are finished with your final draft, place it in the envelope that your teacher will give you. Properly address the envelope.
- Be prepared to read your letter aloud to the rest of the class!

1. Describe who you were and what part you played in the Civil War. _____

_____

_____

_____

2. List two historical facts about the Civil War that you will include in your letter.

　　a. _____

_____

_____

　　Where did you find this fact?_____

　　b. _____

_____

_____

　　Where did you find this fact? _____

3. Describe an exciting or dangerous event that you will include in your letter. _____

_____

_____

_____

4. Who will you send your letter to? Explain why you have chosen this person.

_____

_____

_____

Directions:

- Use your scissors to cut out the envelope along the **bold** black lines.
- Fold the envelope along the dotted black lines.
- Slip your letter inside the envelope, and seal the back of it with a single piece of tape or a sticker.

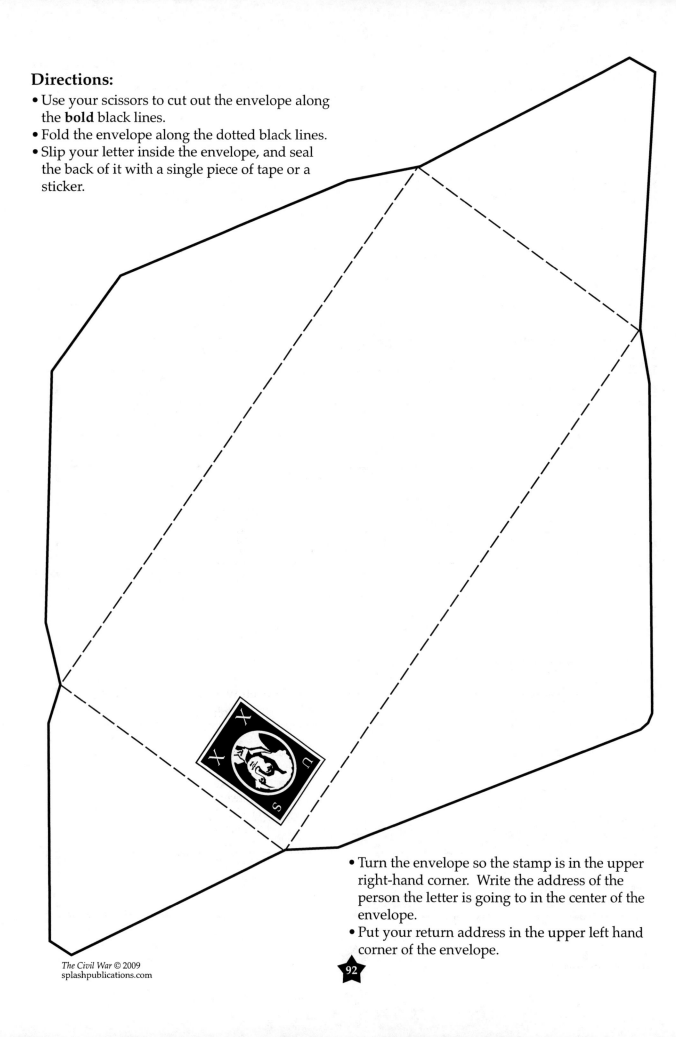

- Turn the envelope so the stamp is in the upper right-hand corner. Write the address of the person the letter is going to in the center of the envelope.
- Put your return address in the upper left hand corner of the envelope.

THE END OF THE CIVIL WAR

By the beginning of 1865, the Confederacy had only 196,000 soldiers ready for battle. President Jefferson Davis sent Vice President Alexander Stephens to meet with President Lincoln and discuss a plan for peace. The meeting did not go well. President Lincoln refused to talk about peace unless the Confederacy agreed to return to the Union and accept the end of slavery. The Confederacy was unwilling to give into President Lincoln's demands.

THE DESTRUCTION OF RICHMOND

General Lee tried a few more times to attack General Grant's army and end the siege at Petersburg. Each time, his forces failed to defeat Grant's Union troops. Finally, General Lee sent word to President Davis that he had to abandon Petersburg. Lee warned that the Confederate government should also leave Richmond.

The Confederate government fled the city, taking government records, important documents, and the treasury's remaining gold. The Confederate soldiers set fire to warehouses with supplies.

Barrels of oil were poured on ships and bridges were burned. Ammunition caught fire and 750,000 shells exploded, killing people everywhere. By the morning of April 3, 1865, a thick cloud of black smoke hung over the city, blocking the sun.

By evening, the first Union troops entered Richmond. Fires were put out and the townspeople who were left were put under military control. Some of the first firemen and policemen in Richmond were black soldiers.

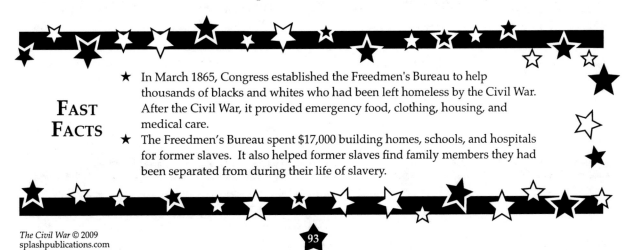

FAST FACTS

★ In March 1865, Congress established the Freedmen's Bureau to help thousands of blacks and whites who had been left homeless by the Civil War. After the Civil War, it provided emergency food, clothing, housing, and medical care.

★ The Freedmen's Bureau spent $17,000 building homes, schools, and hospitals for former slaves. It also helped former slaves find family members they had been separated from during their life of slavery.

Surrender at Appomattox (AP•UH•MAT•TUX)

General Lee's army ran, but they didn't get very far. Lee's men were starving and tired. Union forces were close behind them. By April 6, 1865, more than 7,000 Confederate soldiers and six Confederate generals had been captured. Two days later, the retreating Confederate Army was trapped near the town of Appomattox Court House in Virginia.

General Lee had no choice but to surrender. His army begged him not to give up. "There is nothing left for me to do but to go and see General Grant," he said, "and I would rather die a thousand deaths."

The next day, General Lee rode on horseback into the town of Appomattox Court House where he met with General Grant. General Grant told General Lee the rules for surrendering. All Confederate soldiers were to be treated like **paroled** prisoners. Each soldier could return home as long as he obeyed his parole. Everything except a soldier's horse, gun, and personal property had to be surrendered. Before leaving, General Grant gave General Lee food for his starving soldiers.

The End of the Civil War

Other Confederate armies followed General Lee's example. On April 26, General Joseph Johnston surrendered. On May 4, the Confederate forces in Alabama, Mississippi, and Louisiana surrendered. Three weeks later, the last Confederate troops west of the Mississippi River gave up.

On May 10, 1865, Jefferson Davis was captured. He was arrested and spent the next two years in prison. After four years of fighting, the Civil War was finally over. The American flag once again flew proudly over every state in the nation.

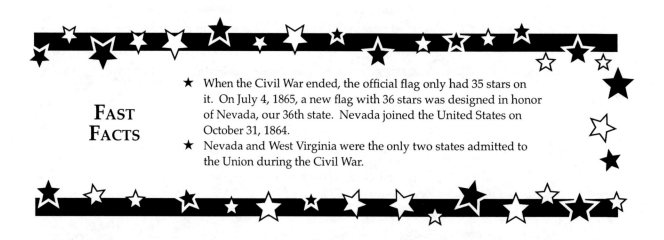

FAST FACTS

★ When the Civil War ended, the official flag only had 35 stars on it. On July 4, 1865, a new flag with 36 stars was designed in honor of Nevada, our 36th state. Nevada joined the United States on October 31, 1864.

★ Nevada and West Virginia were the only two states admitted to the Union during the Civil War.

Name _____

Directions: Read each question carefully. Darken the circle for the correct answer.

1   **Why did President Abraham Lincoln refuse to discuss a plan for peace with the Confederacy?**

   A   President Lincoln wanted to completely crush the Confederacy.

   B   The Confederacy was not willing to return to the Union and accept the end of slavery.

   C   Jefferson Davis wanted to be the president of the United States.

   D   President Lincoln didn't want the Confederate states to rejoin the Union.

2   **Before abandoning Richmond, the Confederates did all of the following except –**

   F   set fire to all of the warehouses

   G   burn the ships and bridges

   H   help the Union Army find all of the important government records

   J   take all of the town's gold

3   **The Freedmen's Bureau was established to –**

   A   help slave owners get their slaves back

   B   help put out the fires in Richmond

   C   help people who needed food, clothing, and medical care after the Civil War

   D   force the Confederate states to free their slaves

4   **What did General Robert E. Lee say he would rather do than surrender to General Grant?**

   F   Die a thousand deaths.

   G   Eat a bug.

   H   Keep fighting.

   J   Sell his horse.

5   **After surrendering, General Grant give General Lee –**

   A   a new uniform

   B   food for his starving army

   C   a horse

   D   ammunition for his gun

6   **Which of the following is an example of a primary source?**

   F   A picture taken of the two generals shaking hands.

   G   The biography of Robert E. Lee.

   H   A drawing of the American flag.

   J   A story about the surrender at Appomattox Court House.

7   **What happened to Jefferson Davis after he was captured?**

   A   He was put to death.

   B   He escaped from the soldiers and lived the rest of his life in California.

   C   He became the president of the United States.

   D   He was sent to prison for two years.

8   **Which two states were admitted to the Union during the Civil War?**

   F   Virginia and Texas

   G   Washington and Nevada

   H   Nevada and West Virginia

   J   West Virginia and Montana

READING

Answers

1   Ⓐ Ⓑ Ⓒ Ⓓ   5   Ⓐ Ⓑ Ⓒ Ⓓ
2   Ⓕ Ⓖ Ⓗ Ⓙ   6   Ⓕ Ⓖ Ⓗ Ⓙ
3   Ⓐ Ⓑ Ⓒ Ⓓ   7   Ⓐ Ⓑ Ⓒ Ⓓ
4   Ⓕ Ⓖ Ⓗ Ⓙ   8   Ⓕ Ⓖ Ⓗ Ⓙ

★ ☆ ☆ ☆ Let's Talk About It ★ ☆ ☆ ☆

The End of the Civil War

After four long years, the Civil War finally ended in 1865. Read the questions below about the end of the Civil War. Write your answers on the lines provided. Attach a separate piece of paper if you need more room. Be ready to discuss some of your answers.

• **President Lincoln refused to talk about peace unless the Confederacy agreed to return to the Union and accept the end of slavery.**

Do you think President Lincoln was too harsh with his demands? In your opinion, do you think it would have been okay for the Confederacy to stay divided from the Union as long as it gave up slavery? Or, would it have been okay to return to the Union and keep slavery? Explain the reasons for your answers.

_____

_____

_____

_____

_____

_____

• **The Civil War was won by the Union.**

Give two examples describing how <u>your</u> life would be different if the Confederacy had won.

1. _____

_____

_____

2. _____

_____

_____

THE DESTRUCTION OF RICHMOND

By the beginning of 1865, the Confederacy had less than 200,000 soldiers ready for battle. President Jefferson Davis sent Vice President Alexander Stephens to meet with President Lincoln. President Lincoln refused to talk about peace unless _____

_____

_____

General Lee tried a few more times to attack General Grant's troops to end the siege at Richmond. A siege is_____

_____

Finally, General Lee sent word to President Davis that he had to _____

Before abandoning Richmond, the Confederate soldiers destroyed the city by _____

_____

One interesting fact about the Destruction of Richmond is _____

_____

_____

_____

_____

JEFFERSON DAVIS

After taking control of Richmond, the Union Army chased after General Robert E. Lee and his Confederate troops. By April 8, 1865, the Confederate Army was trapped near the Virginia town of

_____

General Lee's soldiers begged him not to surrender. Surrender means

_____

Instead of surrendering, General Lee said he would rather _____

_____

According to the rules for surrendering, all Confederate soldiers were to be

treated like _____ prisoners. Each soldier could return

home as long as he _____

Everything except a soldier's_____ , _____ ,

and _____ had to be surrendered. Before leaving,

General Grant gave General Lee_____

On May 10, 1865, _____ was captured. He

was arrested and _____

After ____ years of fighting, the Civil War was finally over. The American flag

once again flew proudly over _____

By now you should have 18 finished pages for your *Civil War Expert's Journal*. Follow the directions below to put the finishing touches on your *Expert's Journal*.

Directions:

1. Look again at each of your *Expert's Journal* pages. Make sure that all of the information has been recorded and all of the pictures have been neatly colored.

2. Arrange your *Expert's Journal* pages neatly on top of each other in this order:

    > *The Battle of Bull Run*
    > *The Battle of Wilson's Creek*
    > *The Battles of Fort Henry and Fort Donelson*
    > *The Battle of Pea Ridge*
    > *The Battle of Shiloh*
    > *The Battle for New Orleans*
    > *The Battle of Yorktown*
    > *The Battle of Fair Oaks*
    > *The Battle of Malvern Hill*
    > *The Second Battle of Bull Run*
    > *The Battle of Antietam*
    > *The Battle of Chancellorsville*
    > *The Battle of Gettysburg*
    > *The Battle of Vicksburg*
    > *The Battle for Atlanta*
    > *Sherman's March to the Sea*
    > *The Destruction of Richmond*
    > *Surrender at Appomattox*

3. Use your coloring pencils to neatly decorate one piece of construction paper for the front cover of your *Civil War Expert's Journal*.

4. Decorate another piece of construction paper for the back cover.

5. Place the front cover on the top and the back cover on the bottom.

6. Staple your *Civil War Expert's Journal* along the left side of the cover.

RECONSTRUCTION

The news of General Robert E. Lee's surrender at Appomattox (ap•uh•MAT•tux) Court House spread like wildfire. People everywhere were sad, angry, and happy, all at the same time. The bitter Civil War lasted four years. Bringing the United States back together would take much longer.

DEATH OF A PRESIDENT

On April 14, 1865, the American flag once again flew over Fort Sumter, South Carolina. Remember, the first shots of the Civil War had been fired by Confederate troops at Fort Sumter. That same night, President Lincoln and his wife went to see a play at Ford's Theater in Washington.

While President Lincoln watched the performance, he was shot in the back of the head by John Wilkes Booth. President Lincoln was carried to a room across the street from the theater. He died the following morning. After his funeral, President Lincoln was buried in Springfield, Illinois.

FORD'S THEATER

ANDREW JOHNSON

Andrew Johnson was a senator in Tennessee when the Civil War broke out. As a Southerner who had spent most of his adult life in Tennessee, Senator Johnson disagreed with the Union's views on slavery. Johnson believed that slaves were property, not people. He didn't think the government had the right to tell people what they could and couldn't do with their personal property.

Although Senator Johnson agreed with slavery, he felt it was wrong for the Southern states to secede from the Union. Senator Johnson tried unsuccessfully to keep Tennessee from becoming a Confederate state. He refused to join Tennessee and become part of the Confederacy. As a result, Andrew Johnson was the only Southern senator to stay loyal to the Union.

Tennessee was a border state between the Union and the Confederate states. More Civil War battles were fought in Tennessee than in any other state except Virginia. In 1862, Union troops took control of Tennessee. President Lincoln put Andrew Johnson in charge of the state.

PRESIDENT JOHNSON

Six months before the end of the Civil War, Abraham Lincoln had been elected president of the United States for a second time. Andrew Johnson was chosen to be President Lincoln's vice president. When President Lincoln was **assassinated**, Vice President Johnson became the president of the United States.

THE RECONSTRUCTION PERIOD

The period after the Civil War was known as **Reconstruction**. Before President Lincoln died, he outlined a plan for putting the nation back together.

Under President Lincoln's plan, the Confederate states were not permitted to rejoin the Union until they agreed to some changes. First, they had to follow the 13th **Amendment** to the Constitution. The 13th Amendment required the Confederate states to free all of their slaves.

The Confederate states were also required to approve the 14th Amendment. This amendment declared all blacks as **citizens** and gave them protection under the law. It also guaranteed blacks a fair trial if they were ever **accused** of a crime.

JOHNSON'S PLAN FOR RECONSTRUCTION

President Johnson did not completely agree with President Lincoln's plan for Reconstruction. He believed that whites should have power over blacks. He also wanted whites to be in complete control of the government.

In order to rejoin the Union, President Johnson simply required the Confederate states to free their slaves and pay for the damage caused by the Civil War. Tennessee was the first Confederate state to **ratify** the 13th Amendment. By the end of 1865, all Confederate states except Texas had ratified the 13th Amendment. President Johnson was satisfied that the Union was once again whole.

PRESIDENT ANDREW JOHNSON

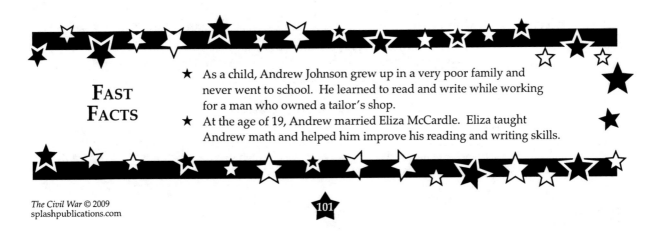

FAST FACTS

★ As a child, Andrew Johnson grew up in a very poor family and never went to school. He learned to read and write while working for a man who owned a tailor's shop.
★ At the age of 19, Andrew married Eliza McCardle. Eliza taught Andrew math and helped him improve his reading and writing skills.

CONGRESS'S PLAN FOR RECONSTRUCTION

Fortunately, the president does not make all of the rules in the United States. The Constitution divides the power of the government into three different branches so that one part of the government, like the president, doesn't become too powerful.

Congress was not satisfied with President Johnson's plan for Reconstruction. The Confederate states would not be permitted to rejoin the Union until they adopted the 14th Amendment and gave blacks the same freedoms and protections as white citizens.

BLACK CODES

Most Confederate states were willing to free their slaves. They were very slow, however, to give blacks the same freedoms and protections as whites. Many Southern states immediately wrote Black Codes. Black Codes kept former slaves from having any real freedom. Blacks in the South were free, but they couldn't vote, own weapons, work and live in white areas, or walk through white neighborhoods without being arrested.

As a result of their stubbornness, Congress removed the Confederate leaders from power and sent soldiers from the Union Army to keep peace and make sure the rules were being followed.

President Johnson tried to keep Congress's plan from working. He made some members of Congress so angry, they tried to have him removed from office.

By 1868, all of the Confederate states except Mississippi, Texas, and Virginia had ratified the 13th and 14th amendments. These three states waited so long to follow the rules that they had to approve these amendments and the 15th Amendment as well. The 15th Amendment granted black men the right to vote. The United States was finally back together as one Union.

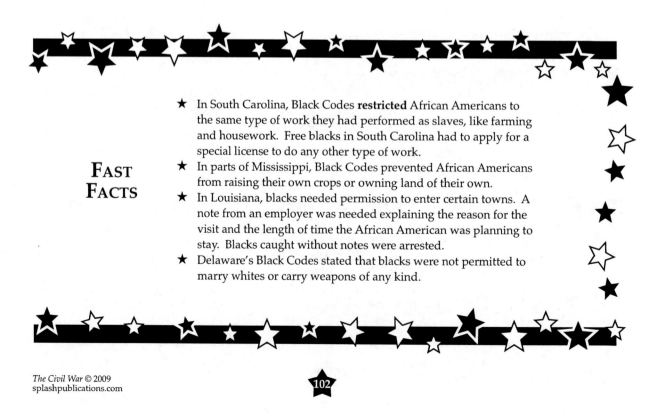

FAST FACTS

★ In South Carolina, Black Codes **restricted** African Americans to the same type of work they had performed as slaves, like farming and housework. Free blacks in South Carolina had to apply for a special license to do any other type of work.

★ In parts of Mississippi, Black Codes prevented African Americans from raising their own crops or owning land of their own.

★ In Louisiana, blacks needed permission to enter certain towns. A note from an employer was needed explaining the reason for the visit and the length of time the African American was planning to stay. Blacks caught without notes were arrested.

★ Delaware's Black Codes stated that blacks were not permitted to marry whites or carry weapons of any kind.

★ ★ ★ RECONSTRUCTION ★ ★ ★

Directions: Read each question carefully. Darken the circle for the correct answer.

1 **What happened to President Lincoln after the Civil War?**

  A He was reelected as president of the United States.

  B He resigned from his presidency to spend more time with his family.

  C He was assassinated.

  D He went to live in South Carolina.

2 **After reading about Andrew Johnson, you get the idea that –**

  F he refused to stay loyal to his state of Tennessee

  G he stayed with the Union because he agreed with the Union's views on slavery

  H he agreed that the South should secede from the Union

  J he was not trusted by President Lincoln

3 **Which of the following describes the 13th Amendment?**

  A Declaring blacks as citizens.

  B Giving whites power over blacks.

  C Setting slaves free.

  D Giving blacks the right to vote.

4 **Which of the following describes the 14th Amendment?**

  F Declaring blacks as citizens.

  G Giving whites power over blacks.

  H Setting slaves free.

  J Giving blacks the right to vote.

5 **Which of the following describes the 15th Amendment?**

  A Declaring blacks as citizens.

  B Giving whites power over blacks.

  C Setting slaves free.

  D Giving blacks the right to vote.

6 **Why did President Johnson disagree with President Lincoln's plan for Reconstruction?**

  F President Johnson didn't think that whites should have power over blacks.

  G President Johnson didn't think the Confederacy should have to rejoin the Union.

  H President Johnson believed that whites should be in complete control of the government.

  J President Johnson wanted to give blacks the freedom to vote.

7 **All of the following are examples of Black Codes except –**

  A blacks were not allowed to own weapons

  B free blacks could live wherever they wanted

  C blacks couldn't walk through white neighborhoods without permission

  D in some states, blacks couldn't raise their own crops or purchase their own land

READING

Answers

1 Ⓐ Ⓑ Ⓒ Ⓓ   5 Ⓐ Ⓑ Ⓒ Ⓓ
2 Ⓕ Ⓖ Ⓗ Ⓙ   6 Ⓕ Ⓖ Ⓗ Ⓙ
3 Ⓐ Ⓑ Ⓒ Ⓓ   7 Ⓐ Ⓑ Ⓒ Ⓓ
4 Ⓕ Ⓖ Ⓗ Ⓙ

Name _____

Take out your Civil War K•W•L•H Chart. Make sure that all of the spaces are filled in on the chart. If necessary, use books from the library, encyclopedias, and the Internet to finish your chart. Read the questions below about the Civil War. Write your answers on the lines provided. Attach a separate piece of paper if you need more room. Be ready to discuss some of your answers.

1   Based on what you have learned about the Civil War, what is the most important <u>new</u> thing you think people should know about the Civil War?

_____

_____

_____

2   Why do you think it is important that people know this about the Civil War?

_____

_____

_____

3   Did your research change what you first thought about the Civil War? Explain the reason for your answer.

_____

_____

_____

4.   If you could ask President Abraham Lincoln one question about the Civil War, what would you ask him?

_____

_____

_____

5.   How do you think President Lincoln would answer your question?

_____

_____

_____

VOCABULARY QUIZ

THE CIVIL WAR
PART IV

Directions: Match the vocabulary word on the left with its definition on the right. Put the letter for the definition on the blank next to the vocabulary word it matches. Use each word and definition only once.

1. _____ former

2. _____ rebellion

3. _____ assault

4. _____ conquered

5. _____ aggressive

6. _____ mill

7. _____ paroled

8. _____ amendment

9. _____ harshly

10. _____ founded

11. _____ demoted

12. _____ ford

13. _____ civilians

14. _____ Emancipation Proclamation

A. change in wording or meaning.

B. approve.

C. a battle against the people who are making unfair rules.

D. a place that has many mountains.

E. defeated by force.

F. people in a city, town, state, or country who enjoy the freedom to vote and participate in government decisions.

G. people who are not part of the military.

H. a building where grain is made into flour and other cereal products.

I. the announcement made by President Abraham Lincoln in 1863, freeing all slaves in the Confederacy.

J. robbed.

K. ditches.

L. unable to live freely.

M. very uncomfortably.

15. _____ assassinated

16. _____ accused

17. _____ plundered

18. _____ citizens

19. _____ peninsula

20. _____ dedication

21. _____ riots

22. _____ ratify

23. _____ siege

24. _____ restricted

25. _____ rally

26. _____ mountainous

27. _____ seaport

28. _____ Reconstruction

29. _____ trenches

30. _____ telegraphed

N. bold and competitive; willing to win no matter what the cost.

O. killed a government leader by a well planned secret attack.

P. a type of ceremony marking the official opening of something important.

Q. to come together for a common cause.

R. blamed or charged with a crime.

S. a large piece of land surrounded by water on three sides.

T. a port, harbor, or town within reach of seagoing ships.

U. a place in a river that can be crossed on foot.

V. sent a message over a system of connected wires.

W. released from prison after agreeing to follow certain rules.

X. reduced to a lower rank.

Y. to surround a city or town and cut it off from receiving supplies and food.

Z. from an earlier time.

AA. started or established.

BB. acts of public violence.

CC. a violent attack.

DD. the period after the Civil War that rejoined the United States as one Union.

GLOSSARY

a•ban•don to leave.

a•bo•li•tion•ists people who fought to end slavery.

ac•cused blamed or charged with a crime.

ad•mired well liked.

ad•van•tag•es favorable positions.

ad•vis•or a person who helps make decisions and gives advice.

ag•gres•sive bold and competitive; willing to win no matter what the cost.

a•mend•ment change in wording or meaning.

am•mu•ni•tion bullets and explosive items used in war.

an•ti•slav•er•y against slavery.

as•sas•si•nat•ed killed a government leader by a well planned secret attack.

as•sault a violent attack.

au•to•bi•og•ra•phy the story of your life written by you.

bales tightly wrapped packages of cotton or hay.

bi•og•ra•phies stories of a person's life written by someone else.

block•ade shutting off a place to keep people and supplies from coming in or going out.

bor•ders lies right next to something.

brig•a•dier gen•er•al a one-star officer in the United States Army who is one rank below a major general.

ca•nals man-made waterways for boats or for watering crops.

can•di•date someone who runs in an election contest.

cap•i•tal the city that serves as the center of government for the state or nation.

Ca•rib•be•an an arm of the Atlantic Ocean surrounded on the north and east by the West Indies, on the south by South America, and on the west by Central America.

cav•al•ry military troops riding on horseback.

cit•i•zens people in a city, town, state, or country who enjoy the freedom to vote and participate in government decisions.

ci•vil•ians people who are not part of the military.

coast an area of land that borders water.

col•o•nies settlements of people who are ruled by another country.

Con•fed•er•ate the nation formed by the 11 Southern states during the Civil War.

con•fi•dent without doubt.

con•flict a struggle or disagreement.

Con•gress the title given to the group of people in the Senate and House of Representatives who are elected to make laws for the United States.

con•quered defeated by force.

con•sti•tu•tion a plan that outlines the duties of the government and guarantees the rights of the people.

con•trast to show the differences.

con•vince talk someone into doing something your way.

de•bate a discussion that gives arguments for and against a subject.

ded•i•ca•tion a type of ceremony marking the official opening of something important.

de•feat•ed won victory over.

de•fend•ing protecting.

de•mot•ed reduced to a lower rank.

e•con•o•my the way a city, state, or country makes money.

e•lect•ed selected leaders by voting for them.

E•man•ci•pa•tion Proc•la•ma•tion the announcement made by President Abraham Lincoln in 1863, freeing all slaves in the Confederacy.

ex•pand grow larger.

fac•to•ries buildings where large amounts of items are produced in the same way at the same time.

fled ran away from danger.

fleet large group of ships.

ford a place in a river that can be crossed on foot.

for•mer from an earlier time.

for•tress a group of forts guarding a city or town.

found•ed started or established.

gen•er•als army officers of one of the five highest ranks.

gov•er•nor a person who is in charge of an area or group.

gun•boats small ships equipped with guns.

har•bor sheltered area of water deep enough to provide ships a place to anchor.

harsh•ly very uncomfortably.

his•to•ri•ans people who study history.

hos•tile very unfriendly.

House of Rep•re•sen•ta•tives one of two groups of people elected to Congress to make laws for our country; the other part of Congress is the Senate.

in•hu•mane without kindness or compassion; unusually cruel.

in•spect•ed carefully checked.

in•sult•ed treated someone badly by calling them names.

in•vade enter an area and take it over by force.

kid•napped took someone without permission.

leg•is•la•ture the branch of government that makes the laws.

lieu•ten•ant the lowest ranking officer in the United States Army.

loy•al faithful.

ma•jor gen•er•al a two-star officer in the United States Army who is one rank below a lieutenant general.

man•u•fac•tur•ing making something from raw materials by hand or machinery.

mil•i•tar•y people who are part of the armed forces who may be asked to go to war.

mi•li•tia a group of people having some military training who are called upon only in emergencies.

mill a building where grain is made into flour and other cereal products.

moun•tain•ous a place that has many mountains.

mus•kets heavy guns used by soldiers.

New World a term once used to describe the continents of North America and South America.

out•num•bered had more people on one side than the other.

out•raged angered beyond belief.

out•ranked had more authority than anyone else.

pan•icked became suddenly filled with fear.

pa•roled released from prison after agreeing to follow certain rules.

pen•in•su•la a large piece of land surrounded by water on three sides.

plan•ta•tion a very large farm in the South where crops of cotton and tobacco were grown and slave labor was usually used.

plun•dered robbed.

pop•u•la•tion the number of people living in a place.

port a city or town located next to water with an area for loading and unloading ships.

Po•to•mac a river that flows southeast from West Virginia to the Chesapeake Bay.

pro•fit•a•ble a type of business that makes more money than it spends.

pro•mot•ed moved up in rank.

raged continued with great violence.

raids sudden attacks.

ral•ly to come together for a common cause.

rat•i•fy approve.

reb•el a person who fights against the government of his or her own country.

re•bel•lion a battle against the people who are making unfair rules.

Re•con•struc•tion the period after the Civil War that rejoined the United States as one Union.

re•cruit to find people who are willing to join a military force.

re•in•force•ments more soldiers sent to help win a battle.

re•signed quit.

re•strict•ed unable to live freely.

re•tired left a job permanently to rest or try something else.

re•treat to back away.

Rev•o•lu•tion•ar•y War battle for independence between the English colonists in America and Great Britain.

ri•ots acts of public violence.

sea•port a port, harbor, or town within reach of seagoing ships.

se•cede withdraw from the Union.

sen•a•tor a member of the Senate, one of two groups of people elected to Congress to make laws for our country.

siege to surround a city or town and cut it off from receiving supplies and food.

so•ci•e•ties groups of people who come together for a common cause.

steam•boat a boat that is powered by a steam engine.

strat•e•gy plan of attack.

strong•hold a well protected area.

su•per•in•ten•dent a person who is in charge.

sur•ren•der to give up completely.

tel•e•graphed sent a message over a system of connected wires.

ter•rain the surface features of a piece of land.

tol•er•at•ed put up with as long as possible.

trans•port move products or people from one place to another.

trench•es ditches.

ves•sels large boats.

vet•er•an a person who has served time in the military.

vowed promised.

voy•age journey that is usually made by water.

ANSWERS

ANSWERS TO COMPREHENSION QUESTIONS

A NATION DIVIDED

1. A
2. F
3. C
4. J
5. B
6. J
7. C
8. G

THE CONFEDERATE ARMY

1. C
2. G
3. A
4. F
5. D
6. G

THE UNION ARMY

1. D
2. G
3. C
4. G
5. C
6. J

THE BATTLE OF BULL RUN

1. B
2. F
3. D
4. H
5. C
6. F
7. B

THE WESTERN THEATER

1. B
2. H
3. C
4. H
5. D
6. F

THE BATTLE OF SHILOH

1. B
2. H
3. A
4. G
5. D
6. H

THE BATTLE FOR NEW ORLEANS

1. C
2. J
3. D
4. J
5. C
6. J
7. A

THE EASTERN THEATER

1. A
2. F
3. C
4. H
5. C
6. F

INVASION OF THE NORTH

1. C
2. J
3. C
4. H
5. D
6. G

BATTLES OF 1863

1. C
2. G
3. D
4. F
5. D
6. F
7. B

BATTLES OF 1864

1. D
2. H
3. D
4. F
5. C
6. F
7. C

THE END OF THE CIVIL WAR

1. B
2. H
3. C
4. F
5. B
6. F
7. D
8. H

RECONSTRUCTION

1. C
2. F
3. C
4. F
5. D
6. H
7. B

ANSWERS TO VOCABULARY QUIZZES

PART I	PART II	PART III	PART IV
1. X	1. H	1. T	1. Z
2. M	2. J	2. H	2. C
3. B	3. M	3. B	3. CC
4. A	4. R	4. P	4. E
5. FF	5. C	5. D	5. N
6. O	6. CC	6. U	6. H
7. I	7. W	7. W	7. W
8. W	8. A	8. A	8. A
9. Q	9. AA	9. M	9. M
10. D	10. E	10. L	10. AA
11. S	11. X	11. I	11. X
12. AA	12. F	12. O	12. U
13. F	13. D	13. R	13. G
14. II	14. T	14. J	14. I
15. U	15. FF	15. C	15. O
16. G	16. U	16. V	16. R
17. K	17. B	17. F	17. J
18. DD	18. N	18. Q	18. F
19. N	19. DD	19. N	19. S
20. H	20. O	20. G	20. P
21. J	21. GG	21. S	21. BB
22. HH	22. S	22. E	22. B
23. CC	23. BB	23. K	23. Y
24. BB	24. Y		24. L
25. R	25. P		25. Q
26. V	26. Z		26. D
27. EE	27. Q		27. T
28. C	28. K		28. DD
29. Y	29. EE		29. K
30. GG	30. L		30. V
31. T	31. G		
32. P	32. I		
33. Z	33. V		
34. L			
35. E			

ANSWERS TO CONSIDER THE SOURCE

1. S	5. P
2. P	6. P
3. S	7. S
4. P	

K•W•L•H Grading Chart

CRITERIA	POINTS POSSIBLE	POINTS EARNED
Answering 3 Questions Before Beginning Research	**15** (5 points each)	
Completing 4 Sections of K-W-L-H Chart (What I **Know**, What I **Want** to Know, What I **Learned**, **How** I Found Out)	**60** (15 points each)	
Answering 5 Questions After Finishing Research	**25** (5 points each)	
TOTAL	**100**	

Persuasive Letter Grading Chart

CRITERIA	POINTS POSSIBLE	POINTS EARNED
Answered each of 6 prewriting Questions	**60** (10 points per question)	
Letter Elements (heading, greeting, body, closing, signature)	**20** (4 points each)	
Makes Persuasive Argument	**15**	
Orally Reads Letter	**5**	
TOTAL	**100**	

Letter Mechanics Grading Chart

CRITERIA	POINTS POSSIBLE	POINTS EARNED
Spelling	12	
Punctuation	12	
Grammar	12	
Capitalization	12	
Sentence Structure	12	
Heading	5	
Greeting	5	
Body (indent)	5	
Closing	5	
Signature	5	
Addressing Envelope	15	
TOTAL	**100**	

UNION/CONFEDERACY PARAGRAPH GRADING CHART

CRITERIA	POINTS POSSIBLE	POINTS EARNED
Topic Sentence	15	
Four Supporting Sentences with appropriate information from Graphic Organizer	60 (15 points per sentence)	
Closing Sentence	15	
Neatness of Final Draft	10	
TOTAL	**100**	

PARAGRAPH MECHANICS GRADING CHART

CRITERIA	POINTS POSSIBLE	POINTS EARNED
Spelling	20	
Punctuation	20	
Grammar	20	
Capitalization	20	
Sentence Structure	20	
TOTAL	**100**	

ANSWERS TO CIVIL WAR EXPERT'S JOURNAL

THE BATTLE OF BULL RUN
The Battle of Bull Run was the first major battle of the Civil War fought in <u>Virginia</u>. The Union's goal during the Battle of Bull Run was to <u>take control of the Confederacy's capital in Richmond</u>. The Union soldiers were led by <u>General Irvin McDowell</u>. The Confederate troops were led by <u>Thomas Jackson</u>. During the battle, Thomas Jackson received the nickname <u>Thomas "Stonewall" Jackson</u> because <u>the Confederate soldiers had stood "like a stone wall."</u> Victory for the Battle of Bull Run went to <u>the</u> <u>Confederacy</u>.

THE BATTLE OF WILSON'S CREEK
Missouri's governor, Claiborne Fox Jackson, wanted his state to <u>secede</u>. Governor Jackson refused to send troops to the <u>Union Army</u>. Montgomery Blair, a Missouri congressman, organized a group of Union volunteers that included <u>a</u> <u>large number of Germans who were against slavery</u>. Blair's Union volunteers were under the command of <u>Captain Nathaniel Lyon</u>. In August 1861, the Battle of Wilson's Creek found General Lyon and his Union troops outnumbered by the Confederate soldiers. Outnumbered means <u>had more</u> <u>people on one side than the other</u>. During the Battle of Wilson's Creek, the Confederate soldiers were led by <u>Sterling Price</u>. Victory for the Battle of Wilson's Creek went to <u>the</u> <u>Confederacy</u>.

THE BATTLES OF FORT HENRY AND FORT DONELSON
Fort Henry was a Confederate fort built on the banks of the <u>Tennessee</u> River. Fort Donelson was a Confederate fort built on the <u>Cumberland</u> River. If the Union could take control of these Confederate forts, <u>the Confederacy would be cut</u> <u>in half and keep Kentucky under control of the Union</u>. During the Battles of Fort Henry and For Donelson, the Union troops were led by <u>General Ulysses S. Grant</u>. The Confederate troops were led by <u>General Lloyd Tilghman</u> and <u>John B. Floyd</u>. Victory for the Battles of Fort Henry and Fort Donelson went to <u>the Union</u>.

THE BATTLE OF PEA RIDGE
While General Grant and his Union troops were capturing Fort Henry and Fort Donelson, the Confederate Army made plans to take complete control of <u>Missouri</u>. During the Battle of Pea Ridge, the Union troops were led by <u>General Samuel</u> <u>R. Curtis</u>. The Confederate troops were led by <u>Sterling Price</u> and <u>General Earl Van Dorn</u> and <u>General Ben McCulloch</u>. The first shots of the Battle of Pea Ridge were fired by <u>the Union</u>. Victory for the Battle of Pea Ridge went to <u>the Union</u>.

THE BATTLE OF SHILOH
Early in April 1862, General Ulysses S. Grant moved his army of 42,000 men to the western banks of the <u>Tennessee</u> River. He was waiting for General Don Carlos Buell to arrive with <u>25,000 Union reinforcements</u>. General Grant was worried because <u>he had his men in the heart of Confederate territory</u>. Just south of General Grant's troops, a Confederate force of 50,000 was protecting <u>the railroad in Memphis, Tennessee</u>. During the Battle of Shiloh, the Union troops were led by <u>General Grant</u>. The Confederate troops were led by <u>General Albert Johnston</u>. Victory for the Battle of Shiloh went to <u>the Union</u>.

THE BATTLE FOR NEW ORLEANS
New Orleans was the largest of the Confederate cities. The Confederacy used New Orleans to <u>ship and receive</u> <u>important products from other states in the South and the Caribbean</u>. As the Union gained control of the Mississippi River, the Confederacy <u>was cut off from New Orleans, its</u> <u>most important city</u>. Fort Jackson and Fort St. Philip were controlled by the <u>Confederacy</u>. During the Battle for New Orleans, the Union troops were led by <u>David G. Farragut</u>. Confederate volunteers in New Orleans were led by <u>General Mansfield Lovell</u>. Victory for the Battle for New Orleans went to <u>the Union</u>.

THE BATTLE OF YORKTOWN
Since the beginning of the Civil War, the Union's goal was to <u>capture the Confederacy's capital in Richmond, Virginia</u>. During the Battle of Yorktown, the Union troops were led by <u>General George McClellan</u>. The Confederate troops were led by <u>General John Magruder</u>. The Confederates tricked the Union into thinking there were more soldiers guarding Yorktown by <u>repeatedly firing their guns and cannons and</u> <u>playing their instruments at one site before quickly moving</u> <u>and playing at another site</u>. Instead of attacking, the Union leader telegraphed President Lincoln and told him <u>that the</u> <u>Confederacy had more than 100,000 soldiers protecting</u> <u>the capital</u>. Victory for the Battle of Yorktown went to <u>the</u> <u>Confederacy</u>.

THE BATTLE OF FAIR OAKS
One month after the Battle of Yorktown, General George B. McClellan was ready to try again to <u>capture the Confederacy's</u> <u>capital</u>. Five miles from Richmond, General McClellan panicked because <u>he realized that the 40,000 troops from</u> <u>Washington never arrived</u>. During the Battle of Fair Oaks, the Union troops were led by General McClellan. The Confederate troops were led by <u>General Johnston</u>. Victory for the Battle of Fair Oaks went to <u>neither the Confederacy or the Union</u>.

THE BATTLE OF MALVERN HILL
The Union believed that defending Malvern Hill would be easy because <u>a swamp at the base of the hill kept the Confederate forces from spreading out</u>. During the Battle of Malvern Hill, the Union troops were led by <u>Major General Fitz Porter</u>. The Confederate troops were led by <u>General Robert E. Lee</u>. Victory for the Battle of Malvern Hill went to <u>the Union</u>. Historians believe the biggest mistake made by the Union after the battle was <u>allowing General Lee and his</u> <u>Confederate troops to return to Richmond</u>.

THE SECOND BATTLE OF BULL RUN
After the Battle of Cedar Mountain, the Confederate troops were found near <u>the former Bull Run battle site</u>. Union General John Pope thought a battle would be quick because <u>the Union troops outnumbered the Confederate troops</u>. General Pope didn't know it at the time, but <u>General Lee's</u> <u>troops had joined Jackson's Confederate forces</u>. During the second day of battle, the Union was surprised by <u>30,000 fresh</u> <u>Confederate soldiers</u>. Victory for the Second Battle of Bull Run went to <u>the Confederacy</u>.

THE BATTLE OF ANTIETAM

On September 16, 1862, Confederate troops moved into position north and east of Sharpsburg in the state of Maryland. They were hiding in the woods, a cornfield, a sunken roadway, and a bridge. At the end of the first day of the Battle of Antietam, the Union was forced to retreat. The Union troops were led by General McClellan. The Confederate troops were led by General Lee. Victory for the Battle of Antietam went to the Union.

THE BATTLE OF CHANCELLORSVILLE

After replacing General George McClellan with General Ambrose Burnside, President Lincoln finally settled on Major General Joseph Hooker. This leader's aggressive style of fighting earned him the nickname "Fighting Joe". During the Battle of Chancellorsville, the Confederate troops were led by General Lee. He split his army into two pieces and sent a large part of his troops with Thomas "Stonewall" Jackson to meet up with the Union Army. Victory for the Battle of Chancellorsville went to the Confederacy.

THE BATTLE OF GETTYSBURG

The Battle of Chancellorsville gave General Robert E. Lee the confidence to once again invade the North. In July 1863, the Confederate and Union armies met in Gettysburg, Pennsylvania. The Union troops were led by General George Gordon Meade. The Confederate troops were led by General Robert E. Lee. By the end of the third day of fighting, victory for the Battle of Gettysburg belonged to the Union. Instead of crushing the Confederate Army, the Union commander refused to continue the attack against the weakened Confederate troops. After the Battle of Gettysburg, President Lincoln gave his famous speech entitled The Gettysburg Address.

THE BATTLE OF VICKSBURG

While the Battle of Gettysburg was raging in Pennsylvania, an important battle was taking place in Vicksburg, Mississippi. Vicksburg was important because it was located right on the Mississippi River. Complete control of the Mississippi River was necessary to win the war. To gain control of Vicksburg, the Union Army surrounded and bombed the small town. Without a way to get food and supplies, the people of Vicksburg began to starve to death.

THE BATTLES FOR ATLANTA

In May 1864, more than 100,000 Union troops headed toward Atlanta, Georgia. Gaining control of Atlanta was important to the Union because it was the Confederacy's most important railroad and manufacturing center. Along the way to Atlanta, Union troops destroyed crops and killed farm animals so the Confederacy would have no way to feed its troops. The Union troops were led by General William Tecumseh Sherman. The Confederate soldiers were led by General Johnston. By September 2, 1864, the city of Atlanta was in complete control of the Union.

SHERMAN'S MARCH TO THE SEA

On November 15, 1864, General Sherman began his famous March to the Sea. As they marched toward Savannah, Sherman's troops were joined by thousands of freed slaves. On December 21, 1864, Sherman and his men reached Savannah, Georgia. They plundered the city. Plundered means robbed. Sherman and his men then turned north and headed into South Carolina. By February 17, 1865, General Sherman had taken control of Columbia, the state's capital. As they had done in Georgia, Sherman's men burned down every Confederate house, barn, and mill that they passed.

THE DESTRUCTION OF RICHMOND

By the beginning of 1865, the Confederacy had less than 200,000 soldiers ready for battle. President Jefferson Davis sent Vice President Alexander Stephens to meet with President Lincoln. President Lincoln refused to talk about peace unless the Confederacy agreed to return to the Union and accept the end of slavery. General Lee tried a few more times to attack General Grant's troops to end the siege at Richmond. A siege is surrounding a city or town and cutting it off from receiving supplies and food. Finally, General Lee sent word to President Davis that he had to abandon Petersburg. Before abandoning Richmond, the Confederate soldiers destroyed the city by setting fire to warehouses, pouring barrels of oil on ships, and burning bridges.

SURRENDER AT APPOMATTOX

After taking control of Richmond, the Union Army chased after General Robert E. Lee and his Confederate troops. By April 8, 1865, the Confederate Army was trapped near the Virginia town of Appomattox Court House. General Lee's soldiers begged him not to surrender. Surrender means to give up completely. Instead of surrendering, General Lee said he would rather die a thousand deaths. According to the rules for surrendering, all Confederate soldiers were to be treated like paroled prisoners. Each soldier could return home as long as he obeyed his parole. Everything except a soldier's horse, gun, and personal property had to be surrendered. Before leaving, General Grant gave General Lee food for his starving soldiers. On May 10, 1865, Jefferson Davis was captured. He was arrested and spent the next two years in prison. After four years of fighting, the Civil War was finally over. The American flag once again flew proudly over every state in the nation.

ANSWERS TO WESTERN THEATER MAPPING

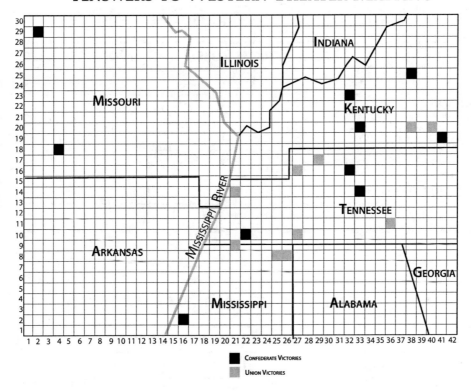

ANSWERS TO EASTERN THEATER MAPPING

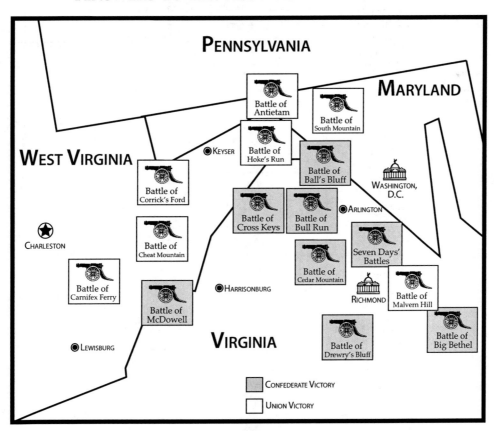

CIVIL WAR LETTER GRADING CHART

CRITERIA	POINTS POSSIBLE	POINTS EARNED
Neatness	10	
Contains at least 2 facts about War	20	
Descriptions of Events	30	
Development of Character	30	
Orally Reading Letter	10	
TOTAL	100	

CIVIL WAR LETTER MECHANICS GRADING CHART

CRITERIA	POINTS POSSIBLE	POINTS EARNED
Spelling	12	
Punctuation	12	
Grammar	12	
Capitalization	12	
Sentence Structure	12	
Heading	5	
Greeting	5	
Body (indent)	5	
Closing	5	
Signature	5	
Addressing Envelope	15	
TOTAL	100	

BIBLIOGRAPHY

All Posters: 'The Underground Railroad Map' 1998 [Online] Available
    <http://www.allposters.com/-sp/The-Underground-Railroad-Map-Posters_i1250871_.htm>
    (April 5, 2008)

American Heritage Dictionary of the English Language, Fourth Edition, Houghton Mifflin,
    Massachusetts, 2000.

Anderson, Dale (2004), *The Causes of the Civil War,* World Almanac Library, Wisconsin

Anderson, Dale (2004), *The Civil War at Sea,* World Almanac Library, Wisconsin

Anderson, Dale (2004), *The Civil War in the East (1861-July 1863),* World Almanac Library, Wisconsin

Beller, Susan Provost (2003), *American Voices From the Civil War,* Benchmark Books, New York

Collier, Christopher and James Lincoln (2000), *Slavery and the Coming of the Civil War,* Benchmark Books,
    New York

Drury, Ian (1993), *Confederate Infantryman 1861-1865,* Osprey, United Kingdom

Flanagan, Timothy (2005), *Reconstruction, A Primary Source History of the Struggle to Unite the North and
    South After the Civil War,* The Rosen Publishing Group, Inc., New York

Ford, Carin T. (2004), *Slavery and the Underground Railroad,* Enslow Publishers, New Jersey

Gay, Kathlyn and Martin (1995), *Voices From the Past: Civil War,* Twenty-First Century Books,
    Connecticut

Handbook of Texas Online: 'Freedman's Bureau' 2008 [Online] Available
    <http://www.tshaonline.org/handbook/online/articles/FF/ncf1.html> (January 5, 2008)

Harper's Weekly: 'The Civil War' 2003 [Online] Available
    <http://www.sonofthesouth.net/leefoundation/the-civil-war.htm> (June 3, 2008)

Harris, Angela: 'Facts About the Gettysburg Address by Abraham Lincoln' 2006 [Online] Available
    <http://hubpages.com/hub/The_Gettysburg_Address_by_Abraham_Lincoln> (June 4, 2008)

Hatt, Christine (1997), *Slavery From Africa to the Americas,* Peter Bedrick Books, New York

Headley, Amy and Smith, Victoria. (2003), *Do American History!* Splash! Publications, Arizona

Heritage Preservation Services: 'Fort Donelson' [Online] Available
    <http://www.nps.gov/hps/abpp/battles/tn002.htm> (October 4, 2008)

Kallen, Stuart (2001), *Days of Slavery,* Abdo Publishing, Minnesota

Kent, Zachary (1989), *Encyclopedia of Presidents: Ulysses S. Grant,* Children's Press, Chicago

Marrin, Albert (1994), *Virginia's General: Robert E. Lee and the Civil War,* Simon & Schuster, New York

Meives, Diane: 'Little Known Facts About Ulysses S. Grant' 2008 [Online] Available
    <http://faculty.css.edu/mkelsey/usgrant/facts.html> (June 9, 2008)

MSN Encarta: 'Major Battles of the Civil War' 2008 [Online] Available
    <http://encarta.msn.com/media_701500524_761569254_-1_1/major_battles_in_the_american_
    civil_war.html> (August 3, 2008)

National Archives, The: 'Black Soldiers in the Civil War' 1999 [Online] Available
    <http://www.archives.gov/education/lessons/blacks-civil-war/> (June 8, 2008)

Stanchak, John (2000), *Civil War,* Dorling Kindersly, New York

White House, The: 'Abraham Lincoln' 2008 [Online] Available
    <http://www.whitehouse.gov/history/presidents/al16.html> (September 3, 2008)